TLP
1.00

Raising
With The
Moon

The Complete Guide
to Gardening
– and Living –
by the Signs of the Moon

Jack R. Pyle
and
Taylor Reese

Copyright 1993 by Jack R. Pyle and Taylor Reese

First Printing, April, 1993
Second Printing, July, 1993

All rights reserved.
No part of this book may be reproduced
by any means without permission of the publisher,
except for brief passages in reviews and articles.

ISBN 1-878086-18-9

Library of Congress Cataloging-in-Publication Data
93-070246

Printed in the United States of America

Cover design by Tim Rickard
Book design by Elizabeth House

Down Home Press
P.O. Box 4126
Asheboro, N.C. 27204

Raising

with the

Moon

To everything there is a season,
and a time to every purpose under the heaven.

A time to be born, and a time to die,
a time to plant
and a time to pluck up that which is planted;

A time to kill, and a time to heal;
a time to break down and a time to build up....

Ecclesiastes 3:1-3

Dedicated to Beth, Dot, Elizabeth and Jerry; to our fellow members of the Writers' Guild of Western North Carolina; and, to the writers of The Mayland Group.

JRP and TR

Contents

Foreword

Our effort here is to give you the full story. We intend to give you the hows and whys of Moon-sign gardening, and a great deal more. The reasons for using the "signs" are never fully explained in other available books, and consequently many people are not aware that the logic behind Moon-sign gardening can also be used in almost every aspect of daily living.

This is a complete one-source reference – a compilation of information from almanacs, old and new. We have searched for the obscure. We have researched and compiled. We wanted to know the reasons behind those brief and often inadequate admonitions found in almanacs.

Planting by the signs had its beginning in antiquity. After thousands of years, the concept is still alive. Why? We are at the dawn of the Twenty-first Century, the age of enlightenment, the age of the computer and space travel, the age of science. Why hasn't the concept died? It continues to live because it works.

The idea of working with Moon signs in a variety of endeavors, well beyond the concept of planting and harvesting, is not a forgotten art. The theories behind it are available, but they must be searched out. This book details it for you without tedious reading, and without the incomplete explanations often found in almanacs.

There is a tendency by the uninformed to treat this subject lightly. Why are some people so free with criticism when they know nothing about the subject, when they speak from total ignorance?

At last, science is beginning to take a genuine interest in both folklore and folk medicine. As they examine and test, they are discovering that a great deal of what is called "lore" has a firm foundation. There is something to "an apple a day" and "mama's chicken soup."

Some scientists were ahead of their times. Here is a quote from Dr. Robert A. Millikan, Nobel Prize Winner (Physics, 1923): "I do know that if man is not affected in some way by the planets, sun and moon, he is the only thing on earth that is not."

Dr. Millikan's concise and engrossing statement went a long way toward serving as an impetus for our writing. We hope his statement, along with this book, will be enlightening and helpful in your life.

Jack R. Pyle/Taylor Reese

Chapter 1
Soil Preparation
Cultivation
Fertilization

This opening chapter is divided into three major aspects of the pre-planting chore: Soil Preparation, Cultivation and Fertilization. Each process is a distinct job, and each requires its own Moon phase and sign, depending on the results desired. For that reason, each division has a thumbnail explanation that embodies the essence of the chapter subsection. We call it The Rule.

The moon passes into a new sign approximately every two and a half days. You will need an almanac or calendar to tell you when the change occurs. Your location will determine exactly when this happens and you can calculate it by using the instructions in the glossary in the back of this book. The glossary contains complete listings of barren and fruitful signs as well as information about the Moon's four phases.

Soil Preparation

THE RULE: Turn the soil in the 1st or 2nd Quarter (New Moon to Full Moon), in a barren sign, Leo, Gemini or Virgo preferred.

This desirable tilling period (called the Light of the Moon) begins with the New Moon and continues until the Full Moon. It is a time when the Moon is enlarging, growing in light. Because of this expansion, soil can be turned more easily. It will stay light and pulverized. Clods can be raked easily into beds or rows.

Conversely, the 3rd or 4th Quarter (called the Dark of the Moon) represents a time of diminishing lunar energy, since the light decreases with each passing day. It is a time of contraction. Tilling during this period will produce hard clods, compact earth, making your work more difficult. Worse yet, the soil will continue to harden around your plant's root system, slowing growth.

Barren signs are selected for soil preparation for the following reason: Although you till to loosen the soil, you are also uprooting weeds and other unwanted growth. By the use of a barren sign, you are attacking weeds during a period when they are vulnerable, when they are less able to sustain life, because of a damaged or detached root system. Leo is the most destructive of the barren signs, followed by Gemini and Virgo. If these signs cannot be used for soil preparation because of time restrictions, consider Aquarius and Aries, also barren signs, although to a lesser degree.

One-half of each lunar month (or approximately 14 days) is favorable for tilling. It should not be difficult to find a barren sign during the first two quarters (New Moon to Full Moon). Always till on a growing Moon.

Some gardeners prefer Gemini (the twins) for plowing if killing weeds is the prime purpose. Why Gemini over Leo? We considered it. Is it because Gemini is an air sign, and your tilling exposes the roots, so they are quickly dried out and die? This might be an explanation, but if so, would not Leo, a fire sign, do equally well? Wouldn't it, in addition, since Leo is the sign ruling the heart, allow broken parts of the weed to "bleed" and thus hasten its demise?

Gemini is a good choice, but when asked about this theory of Gemini being the most effective of the barren signs for killing weeds, we got replies like this one: "It kills them better, that's all. I try to till in the twins (Gemini)."

What about Virgo, our third choice? We can see she might not be the most "final" sign for killing weeds. It is an earth sign, with a natural affinity to the roots of plants, but Virgo is the virgin, and therefore barren. The value of Virgo is not so much in the killing of unwanted growth but in the fact that she is barren. She will not reproduce. The weed you uproot may be the last of the line.

Cultivation

THE RULE: Hoeing, weeding or tiller cultivation is best done on the 3rd or 4th Quarter of the Moon, in one of the barren signs.

Shallow cultivation with a tiller or hoe, or even weeding by hand, is not concerned with keeping the soil soft down at the root system, as was the case with soil preparation. When you cultivate, you are uprooting weeds or cutting them off, and you are working near the surface. Because of this, you can use both the Moon's phase and a barren sign.

2

By using a waning Moon (from Full Moon to the next New Moon), you are using the time of the Moon's declining energy, which will help in the destruction of weeds. The reason for using a barren sign is obvious: You are destroying unwanted growth, so you choose a sign that does not encourage either growth or re-growth. Any of the barren signs will do: Leo, Gemini, Virgo, Aquarius or Aries. But, if you are hoeing or weeding, where the roots will be cut off or pulled out, we prefer Leo, because there will be more "bleeding," a greater loss of moisture from the cut or tear. The dying process will be hastened by this fire sign.

Fertilization

THE RULE: Apply fertilizer in the 1st (New Moon) or 2nd Quarter of the Moon, when a chemical fertilizer is being used; apply an organic fertilizer in the 3rd (Full Moon) or 4th Quarter. In either case, apply fertilizers in a fruitful sign: Cancer, Scorpio or Pisces preferred.

First, let's look at the Moon's phases and the cleavage between chemical and organic fertilizers. Since they are both intended to produce the same result, why is this so? Chemical fertilizers are used more frequently than organic, and they will be considered first. They are to be used in the 1st (New Moon) and 2nd Quarters. The reason is the nature of the fertilizer. Chemical fertilizers are not in complete harmony with the soil. They are man-made. Therefore, they are not so readily assimilated by the plant. And, being foreign to the plant, the "energized" part of the Moon's cycle promotes the breakdown of the chemicals so that the plant can utilize the benefits provided.

In the instance of organic fertilizers, they are already in a part of nature's cycle. They are already in one of the steps in a revolving cycle that is the natural evolution of plant life. At the time they are applied, these fertilizers are in the process of organic breakdown, and the process will be further hastened by the deteriorating, dying Moon. For that reason, apply organic fertilizers anytime from the Full Moon to the next New Moon (3rd or 4th Quarters), because the waning Moon will add to the evolutionary process, and all natural fertilizers will be more quickly absorbed.

Irrigation

If you have to water your garden, do so in the water signs (Cancer,

Scorpio or Pisces). If this is not possible, use the earth signs Taurus or Capricorn.

Because it is fruit/vegetable growth you are trying to gain from irrigation, the growing phases of the Moon (1st or 2nd Quarters) are preferred over the dying phases (3rd and 4th). Why? The growing phases of the Moon are times when the Moon's energies are available to the plant, allowing a freer intake of moisture.

The phase of the Moon, however, is not the critical factor in watering, but it does aid the process. Any phase of the Moon will do when the necessity to irrigate arises. The important thing is to get the water to the plant. Deep watering is better than frequent shallow watering.

Try to do it when the Moon is in a water sign.

Chapter 2

Planting

THE RULE: Plant when the Moon is in the 1st or 2nd Quarter for crops that produce their yield above ground, and in the 3rd or 4th Quarter for those producing below the ground, in one of the fruitful or semi-fruitful signs.

This general rule is the basic explanation. To be truly useful, both the Moon phase and the sign need further amplification. After the thumbnail descriptions, there will be a complete explanation of each. We want you to understand the reasoning behind The Rule.

The Moon Phases

1st Quarter: For above-ground crops. Best for annuals that produce seed outside the fruit.

2nd Quarter: Also for above-ground crops, any annual that produces seeds inside the fruit.

3rd Quarter: Good for root crops, bulbs, perennials or biennials.

4th Quarter: Same explanation as the 3rd Quarter, but less desirable. Use this Quarter of the Moon only when a 3rd Quarter planting opportunity does not exist.

The Signs

Fruitful signs – the water signs:

Cancer: The most fruitful of the signs. Excellent if production (volume) is the goal. Abundance.

Scorpio: A good sign for sturdiness or vine growth.

Pisces: A good sign for root growth.

Semi-fruitful signs:

Taurus: A sign for quick growth or root crops. Hardiness.

Capricorn: Use when pulp or stalks are desirable.

Libra: Good for flowers (annuals).

There are advantages and disadvantages to both the choice of the Moon phase and the sign, depending on the nature of the item being planted and the results desired.

Use The Rule cited at the beginning of the chapter, but understand the nature of the Moon's phases and signs. Understand how it works and why. Working with nature will produce more and better results than haphazard planting.

First, the Moon's phases in detail and then an examination of the fruitful signs. Each is beneficial in its own application.

The Moon Phases

THE RULE: Above-ground crops do best when planted in the 1st and 2nd Quarters, while below-ground crops need the 3rd and 4th Quarters. Or, to state it another way: above ground in the Light of the Moon, below ground in the Dark of the Moon.

The Rule, however, is very general. In order for you to have complete success, you will need more specific information. The quarters (the Light and the Dark of the Moon) are fully explained in the Glossary. We urge you to review it.

Throughout this book we will be referring to the four quarters of the Moon, just as they occur, beginning with the New Moon and proceeding through the four phases to the next New Moon. Anything from New Moon to Full Moon (the 1st and 2nd Quarters) is considered the light of the Moon; anything from Full Moon to the next New Moon (3rd and 4th Quarters) is considered the Dark of the Moon. With that in mind, let us look at each quarter and each phase of the Moon and its specific usefulness to the gardener.

1st Quarter (New Moon): Plant annuals (those things that grow for one season and then must be re-seeded) that produce their yield above the ground, and specifically those annuals that produce their seed outside the fruit. Many of these will be leafy vegetables, such as lettuce, broccoli, celery. There is an exception: Plant cucumbers in this quarter even though the seed is produced inside the fruit. This is also a good quarter for planting grains: wheat, barley, oats or rye, because they produce their seeds on the outside.

2nd Quarter: This is also for planting annuals (single season plants), but in this quarter plant those vegetables or fruits that produce seed inside the fruit, tomatoes or squash being examples. Other examples of vegetables that should be planted in this phase of the Moon are: peas, beans, eggplant, okra, peppers, pumpkin, to name just a few. This phase, too, is equally as good as the 1st Quarter for the planting of various grains. This seems to go against the seed-inside/seed-outside rule (just as cucumbers did), but all research indicates that either quarter may be used for planting grains.

When planting specifically for seed rather than for eating or canning, plant in the 2nd Quarter of the Moon. This applies to those fruits or vegetables you would normally plant in the 1st Quarter, i.e., those that produce their seeds outside rather than inside, broccoli as an example. If you use this quarter of the Moon, you will produce more and better seeds for your next year's crop. This would be true of flowers planted specifically for seed.

3rd Quarter (Full Moon): Plant all bulbs and root vegetables in this phase of the Moon. This is the proper quarter for perennials, biennials, all trees, shrubs and bushes. And it is the proper quarter for anything planted in the fall for harvest in the spring. It's also the proper time for planting berries or anything that continues to produce from the same root stock: asparagus, rhubarb, strawberries. There has been an unintentional emphasis here on perennials and on those things that continue to produce from the same root stock, but at the risk of repeating, this is also the proper quarter for planting any annual that produces below the surface of the earth: Potatoes, beets, radishes, carrots and other root crops.

4th Quarter: Use this quarter of the Moon for the planting of any of the things listed in the 3rd Quarter, if no other time is available to you, and this can happen to the most experienced gardener. Generally speaking, however, the 4th Quarter might be considered a "non-planting" quarter, because the Moon's energies are at low ebb. It can be a useful quarter for weeding, hoeing, cultivating, and the destroying of pests, and especially if you do your destroying in barren signs: Leo (the heart), Gemini (the twins), Virgo (the virgin), Aquarius (the waterman or water bearer), Sagittarius (the archer) or Aries (the ram). (See additional explanation of this in Chapter 6.)

The Planting Signs

Cancer: The crab, ruling the breast and stomach, a fruitful, water sign. Cancer gives quick germination, good growth and good yield. There is a valid reason: Cancer is ruled by the Moon, so, when the Moon enters the sign, there is a natural affinity. You have a combination of strengths.

The Moon, ruler of Cancer, also rules: germination, dampness (necessary for germination), fruitfulness and the nurturing or maternal instincts of plants or animals. In fact, the Moon is considered the "cosmic mother." With all of this, is it any wonder that Cancer, ruled by the Moon, is the most fruitful of the signs? In addition to planting, the Moon in Cancer is an excellent time for irrigation, budding, grafting or transplanting.

It is also said that pruning just before Full Moon in Cancer will keep insects at a minimum. We offer no explanation, but we know pruning should be done in a fruitful sign so the process will not harm the plant. Insects gravitate to weak plants.

Scorpio: The scorpion, or the eagle, ruling the secrets (genitals), another water sign. The second most fruitful sign, excellent for planting corn. It is ruled by Pluto (co-ruled by Mars). Pluto is the planet of "rebirth," while Mars denotes "action." Pluto, similar to the Moon, aids germination because it rules generation and regeneration. Pluto is the ruler of all those things that die in one form and are reborn in another. A seed dies in one form, but from that germ comes a new plant.

The Moon in Scorpio is ideal for planting or transplanting. While the Moon in Scorpio is considered second to Cancer in fruitfulness, in some instances it is the sign of preference. The Moon in Scorpio will produce good vine growth and sturdy plants. This can be important, depending on what you are planting. Tomatoes, for example, benefit from sturdy stalks or vines. And this could be true of several other vegetables where the fruit can grow heavy before it is ready for harvest.

Pisces: The fishes, ruling the feet, the third of the fruitful water signs. Suitable for all crops, but it is especially good for root crops when they are planted in the proper phase of the Moon (3rd Quarter). The reason is that Pisces is ruled by Neptune which also rules liquids in general. It rules osmosis – that process where water is taken from the earth and brought into the plant – and it rules a variety of other water-related subjects: dew, fog, reservoirs, ponds, foam, sponges, solutions, and even irrigation. It takes moisture for germination, and you can readily see how Pisces fits. The Moon in Pisces activates those water-related things necessary for germination.

Taurus: The bull, rules the neck and throat. It is a semi-fruitful earth sign. This sign is good for root crops, perhaps because it is an earth sign, but it is also good for crops where quick growth is desirable. The reason Taurus is rated No. 4 becomes clear when you realize it is ruled by Venus, which also rules, among other things, procreation, fruitfulness and offspring in general. You can readily see how this ties in. Taurus, though not a water sign, brings with it the element of creation – the changing of a seed into a plant. Venus also rules gardens in general, which accents the affinity even more. Taurus is an excellent sign for planting lettuce, cabbage or any of the leafy vegetables.

Capricorn: The goat, rules the knees, and is the second of the semi-fruitful earth signs. It is a moist sign and will produce rapid growth where root, stalk or pulp are desirable.

Capricorn should not be used for planting grain. It will prove to be a very poor producer even if you plant in the proper phase of the Moon. When grains are planted you are looking for seed and not for heavy stalks or good roots.

Both Taurus and Capricorn are earth signs. You might wonder why Taurus is rated No. 4 and Capricorn No. 5. One explanation is that Capricorn is ruled by Saturn. It is true that Saturn rules farms and farming, a decided plus, but you must also know that it rules a myriad of other things: constraint, barren ground, dryness, regressions, shrinkage, poor circulation, blockades, starvation, barriers.

So you see the connection. Capricorn is an earth sign, but an unforgiving earth sign. There is restriction here. If you use the best seeds, if you put them in the ground properly, if the phase of the Moon is correct, if the ground maintains sufficient moisture, then you could have good growth. BUT, since planting when the Moon is in Capricorn involves Saturn, you must never expect more than is earned. All things must be right. Saturn will not be generous. Capricorn can produce good growth, if that is desired, but it is not overly fruitful.

Libra: The scales, ruling the reins (or kidneys), is a semi-fruitful, movable sign. You may have noted that all previous fruitful or semi-fruitful signs were feminine. Libra is an air sign and the only masculine sign used for planting. So, how does this masculine, air sign even get considered as a good sign for planting? It seems to have everything against it. But Libra has one redeeming feature: It is ruled by Venus, just as Taurus is, and Venus makes it fruitful (to the extent that it is fruitful); the things Venus brings to mind are procreation, the production from a seed, fruitfulness.

This is not, however, a prime sign for planting the general food garden, although it will produce strong roots and good pulp. Libra is excellent for flowers and ornamentals. If beauty is your aim, consider Libra.

There you have it. Planting by the signs is easy. Coordinating the sign and the Moon's phase is also easy, because you have several choices in every month, so you can fit planting into your other scheduled activities.

There is no one way when planting by the Moon's phases or signs. Some are better, but you have wide latitude. Try to choose both the phase and the sign for the specific job at hand. You have a tomato seed, for example. You know it's a heavy producer and you've had trouble with the vines breaking from the weight of the fruit. Try planting in Scorpio or Taurus so the sturdy aspect of the plant will be accented. As planting time approaches, look for the Moon in Scorpio or Taurus, sometime during the 1st or 2nd Quarter (preferably the 2nd Quarter because the seed is produced inside the fruit). If this is not possible, take another alternative. Because you know Pisces will produce a superior root system, it might solve the problem; or, Capricorn, another sign that will produce strength in the foliage.

The point is: *There is no one right way*. First, decide on the phase of the Moon and then find the sign that will best suit your purpose, or best suit the time you have available for gardening.

You will be the final judge of whether or not planting by the Moon's phases and signs will produce as the "sign-gardeners" are already convinced they will. We have had excellent results.

There have been a number of studies done by scientists, under controlled conditions. Here are some remarkable results of one such study done by botanist Dr. Clark Timmons:

1. Marigolds: When sown with the Moon in Cancer, 90 percent germination; with the Moon in Leo, 32 percent.

2. Tomatoes: Sown with the Moon in Cancer, 90 percent germination; with the Moon in Leo, 58 percent.

3. Carrots: When sown with the Moon in Scorpio, 64 percent germination; with the Moon in Sagittarius, only 47 percent.

4. Beets: When sown with the Moon in Scorpio, 71 percent germination; with the Moon in Sagittarius, only 58 percent.

Keep in mind that the above results were not the findings of "just another gardener." These were the results of a scientific experiment, conducted under controlled conditions that eliminated variations in soil type, soil temperature, moisture, etc. This is not meant to be a complete report on Dr. Timmons' findings, but it is representative. Also keep in mind that Dr. Timmons' work is not the only study that has been done or is being done on this subject. There is a considerable body of scientific work that tends to corroborate what "sign gardeners" have known and wisely utilized over the centuries.

One more comment about Dr. Timmons' work as it concerns planting by the phases of the Moon. He transplanted healthy tomato seedlings on an increasing Moon with a 100 percent survival. The same seedlings were transplanted on a decreasing Moon and all died. This was a rather extreme result, for we have done this with less dire consequences. We admit, however, that on the decreasing Moon we did have to replant some of our tomatoes, but not all of them.

Keep this in mind: Our experience was in a garden and not under controlled conditions, so there could have been other factors that gave us a greater percentage of living plants from a decreasing Moon.

When to plant: This, of course, depends on where you live. There is no way you could compare Michigan to Florida, or Georgia to Vermont. We suggest you consult your farm agent, asking when the date of the average last frost occurs in your area. This is information he will have readily available.

However, there are several "natural indicators" gardeners have used over the years, before anyone ever heard of a "county farm agent." Oldtimers will tell you: "When the forsythia shows color, you can safely plant all frost-hardy crops, such as: sweet peas, English peas, cabbage, spinach, radishes, lettuce, onions, carrots; when the spirea is in full bloom it is safe to plant the rest of your garden, the frost-susceptible plants, either flowers or vegetables." Some gardeners ignore the spirea. They are of the opinion that it is not safe to plant any frost-susceptible plants until the lilacs are in bloom.

Before we leave this chapter on Planting there are other interesting observations. A neighbor said, "I never plant on the day of the New or Full Moon." When asked why, there was no ready answer. This might be the explanation: Our calendars, and even some of our almanacs, show the hour the Moon enters the New Moon phase, but sometimes they don't. If you don't know the hour in your area, then planting on the day indicated as the New Moon, or the Full Moon, is risky at best, because you could be planting during the "dead" of the Moon (hours or even minutes before the arrival of the New Moon); or, with the Full Moon, you could be planting root crops in a phase more suitable for above-ground producers.

Example: Your almanac might show the date of the New moon, but if you took the time to find the exact hour of its arrival, you might find it was going to occur at 9 p.m. If you planted on that date but before 9 p.m. (and after nine is an unlikely time for planting), you'd be planting on the last few hours of the waning Moon, a very poor time indeed.

Another example: Assume your almanac does show the exact time of the New Moon. You must ascertain which Standard Time was used in these calculations. Some almanacs indicate the computations were done for the area surrounding Boston, Massachusetts; others will say Eastern Standard Time, or Greenwich Mean Time. To be sure of the time in your area, you will have to make some simple calculations. The instructions are contained in the Glossary.

If you don't mind doing a little figuring, you needn't pay any attention to the admonition often repeated by sign-gardeners of "never plant on the first day of the New or Full Moon," because you'll know exactly when these phenomena will occur in your area.

Remember, once this calculation is made, it will stay the same, so all you have to do is add or subtract from the data given on your planting calendar or almanac. Example: Your planting guide is computed for Eastern Standard Time—or 75 degrees longitude. You live in Columbia, South Carolina, which is 81 degrees longitude. The correction required (details in the Glossary) is the addition of 24 minutes. So, if the Moon will enter Pisces at 8 a.m. EST, you add the 24 minutes of correction. Result: The Moon will enter Pisces at 8:24 a.m. in Columbia, South Carolina, and you can plan your planting chores accordingly.

As previously noted, some gardeners will advise you not to plant on the first day of any Moon change. And, if you don't care to calculate, it's good advice. But if you are willing to make the effort (changing a stated time in your almanac to your local time) then this "rule of experience," this admonition to never plant on the first day of a sign or the first day of a New or Full Moon, may be safely overlooked. It's not just an old wives' tale. It's perfectly valid for those who do not wish to make an accurate calculation.

If you make the computation, keep this in mind: The first day of a sign is better than the second or third. The reason: The strength of the sign wanes as it nears the next sign, just as the strength of the Moon wanes from the Full Moon until it is totally spent.

Another comment often heard: "Plant your flowers in the sign of the scales (Libra). That's where they do best." And why not? Venus rules flowers, fragrances, beauty, and even one's reaction to beauty. Why wouldn't this be an excellent sign?

Along this line, we have found many people who think Libra is the only sign – or certainly the best sign – for planting pumpkins or gourds. Is this because pumpkins and gourds are ornamental? Possibly.

However, whether you plant your flowers or pumpkins in Libra or choose to plant them in one of the more fruitful signs, be sure you choose the correct phase of the Moon. If the seeds form inside the fruit (pumpkin), use the 2nd Quarter; if they form outside (marigold, for example), use the 1st Quarter of the Moon.

One more comment about flowers: If you are planting in Libra for beauty and fragrance (the primary purpose of flowers), keep in mind that this sign will produce fewer leaves and fewer seeds. Flowers planted in Pisces or Cancer will produce more abundantly (perhaps not so beautifully or fragrantly) and will also produce more seed for planting next year. Many people have a strong preference for Pisces for flowers. It gives strong roots, vigorous plants and abundant flowers. The opinion is valid.

What about lawns?

If you think about it, a lawn is a perennial. It grows on the same rootstock year after year. As such, it should be planted in a fruitful sign in the 3rd Quarter of the Moon. While it is true that the grass part grows above the ground – the part you normally think about when you think of your lawn – it's still a fact that it is "growing on the same rootstock year after year." It is definitely a perennial. It should be planted in the correct Moon phase in order to achieve its full beauty. Without a good root system, your lawn can't amount to much.

Some joker said, "Never plant anything in the sign of Gemini. This is an air sign, good only for the planting of ideas." On the face of it, the quote has validity. Gemini is an excellent time for contemplation, but it has more plebeian uses: It's a good time to plow weeds under, to hoe, to weed or to cultivate, especially in the 4th Quarter of the Moon.

Planting by the signs and phases of the Moon is an interesting subject, with basic rules, but, as you've seen, there are variations in those rules, depending on the gardener and his past experience. Where we garden, in the beautiful mountains of Western North Carolina, you find a strain of people who won't hold still for all of the rules. They are fiercely independent, being the progeny of adventurers who had the courage to settle in these mountains when they were completely isolated, when roads were the merest of trails, and when taking your produce to market was a two- or three-day journey each way.

Here in the mountains (and perhaps elsewhere) you will hear many sign-gardeners, good gardeners, real producers, say: "I plant my beans in the twins (Gemini). They produce better. I have all the beans I can use and some to give away." This, of course, flies directly in the face of The Rules. Gemini is barren and ought not to be used for planting.

But we frequently hear this preference for Gemini, and it seems to be specifically for beans. Gemini is a mutable (negative) sign, an air sign, therefore, less destructive than fire signs; and it is the sign of the twins, a dual sign, and, as such, possibly it could offer multiple blooms. If your beans are going to produce at all, you would require a great volume of blooms, since each unit, when cooked, is no more than a forkful. And Gemini rules the arms – the tentacles of a bean vine. Could this be a reason for the preference?

Other than these rather weak suggestions, we have no explanation of why some prefer the twins "for my beans."

In addition to hearing the preference for planting beans in the twins, we've read it. We found it in one of the most popular almanacs eight or ten years ago. So the idea is not purely local. But, to us, this use of the twins presents a real paradox, because Gemini, by all accounts, is barren, the second most destructive sign for planting.

What is our advice? Experiment, if you wish, or simply stick to the basics. We prefer to avoid Gemini for any type of planting, in favor of a more fruitful sign. In the case of beans specifically, we will take the Moon in Cancer as a first choice, in the 2nd Quarter.

But, while we are on this Gemini phenomenon, we should make it clear that it is a sign favored by many people for cucumbers, melons – even watermelons – in the Southeastern states, where the growing season is longer.

Keep this point in mind: In all of the research we've done, the overwhelming consensus is that Gemini is suitable only for "stirring the soil to kill unwanted growth, cutting weeds or pulling them out, mowing the lawn or trimming shrubs to slow down growth."

While we are discussing local customs, there are many sign-gardeners here in western North Carolina who say, "I always plant my potatoes on Good Friday." They give no explanation for this. They just make that flat statement.

It aroused our curiosity. Was this practice based on a religious belief, or was this, too, "sign-gardening"? Since Easter is always the Sunday following the first Full Moon that occurs on or after March 21, we know at once that Good Friday (the Friday before Easter) will always occur in the 3rd Quarter, since it follows a Full Moon. The 3rd Quarter, the "dark of the Moon," is ideal for planting root crops.

The Moon's sign, of course, will vary since the date Good Friday falls on – even the month – varies. But we looked at the 25-year period from 1960 through 1985. The Moon was in a fruitful or semi-fruitful sign nearly 70 percent of the time. We do not think such a percentage would be accurate for other 25-year periods. If you should elect to plant potatoes on Good Friday, the only thing you can really rely on is that the Moon's phase will always be correct.

Now, let's look at Good Friday from a practical point of view. Easter can fall in March. In some areas this would be entirely too early to plant anything. In some areas the ground would still be frozen. Accordingly, this might be a reasonably good day for planting your potatoes, but only if the climate permits.

Now, you might well ask: "If you are such a stick in the mud and only go with the most fruitful signs, how are you ever to know you couldn't have had just as healthy and abundant a crop in some other sign?"

We haven't always gardened by the signs; we haven't always known enough about them. It's one thing to remember your father or grandfather with the almanac in his hand as he planned his garden, but you did not – or we did not – always know what they were doing. Gardening by the signs is a newly-found practice with us. And, yes, we have experimented with it. We have both deliberately and accidentally planted in barren signs, and also in incorrect phases of the Moon, so experience has been our teacher. We keep a garden diary. We know for each garden year when we planted, the sign, whether it was the first, second or the third day into the sign, and we have a record of the results. We have learned by this experience. If you don't learn by experience, the effort has been wasted.

Try your own experiments. We recommend it. It's not all cut and dried. There are rules and exceptions. We want to make you aware of all the variations.

For example: The five most fruitful signs are all feminine. This makes sense, since the feminine gender comprises the mothers of the earth, almost without exception. But, even here, there is variation. Virgo is a feminine sign; it's an earth sign, just as Taurus and Capricorn are, and logic would say that it should, therefore, be, at the very least, semi-fruitful. This is not so.

Virgo is the third most valuable sign for destroying unwanted growth. Why should there be such an exception? We, too, gave this considerable thought, and we tried to search out the reasons. We offer this information: Virgo, the virgin, certainly would *not* represent motherhood and as such would *not* tend to produce. Virgo rules the bowels, which suggest excretion or elimination and not the contrary. Virgo rules bowel troubles, too, which would include a myriad of things: constipation, diarrhea, cramps, dysentery; and these suggest anything other than growth. Virgo rules disease, a debilitating factor, and Virgo rules the toenails, the "non-living" part of the human body.

Yes, Virgo is a feminine sign, but the fact that it is also a barren sign seems to overshadow all other considerations, especially if we are seeking to produce, to give birth, to make a seed form life.

We should stress one exception before Virgo is completely blasted out of the box as a planting sign: It will not produce vegetables in your garden. But it is suitable for planting shade trees or leafy ornamentals. It will make good foliage – plenty of show, but no production.

Nor is Virgo the only anomaly. Masculine signs tend to be barren, but Libra is the exception. This has been previously mentioned so we won't dwell on it. One wonders why this is the case. Is it because Libra is a movable air sign? Does this make it less lethal than either Gemini or Aquarius? Perhaps. Any air sign would be better than the three fire signs of Leo, Sagittarius and Aries. Or, could it be because some of the masculinity is mitigated by the kinds of things Libra (Venus) rules? Beauty is the first thought, and flowers the second, but there are other things that make one think quickly of reproduction: love, lovers, loins, ovaries, partners, weddings, harmony, bedrooms, just to name a few.

To the basic rule for planting, those are the two bona fide exceptions; Virgo is a feminine sign, yet it is barren; Libra is a masculine sign, yet it is semi-fruitful.

One last thought concerning planting in general, and specifically concerning the planting of seeds rather than plants. Plant as early in the day as possible, so the growing energy of the Sun can begin the process of germination. Always try to work with nature's growing or ebbing energies, depending on the result you are trying to achieve.

At the end of this chapter you will find an alphabetical Planting Guide showing preferred Moon phases, and preferred, or at least suitable, signs for planting. This may not be a complete listing of the things you want in your garden, but it is representative. You should be able to figure both the phase and the sign for any unlisted vegetable. A sunflower, for example, is not listed, and it certainly does have a place in many gardens. Think about it. You know it produces above ground, and the seeds are on the outside, so we know at once that the New Moon (1st Quarter) would be the best phase, and since we're planting rather than destroying, we know that any of the fruitful or semi-fruitful signs will do. For abundance, we might use Cancer; for sturdiness, Scorpio; for a strong root system – good for such a tall plant – Pisces; for hardiness, Taurus. And if the purpose is simply to add beauty or charm to the garden, Libra would be a good choice.

The point is, the Planting Guide and the contents of this chapter should give you plenty of clues so that you might select suitable signs and Moon phases for any of the more esoteric garden or farm products that have not been specifically listed.

Chart 1 – A Planting Guide

Name	Moon Phase	Suitable Sign for Planting
Asparagus	3rd	Cancer, Scorpio, Pisces
Barley	1st (2nd)	Cancer, Scorpio, Pisces, Libra, Capricorn
Beans	2nd (1st)	Cancer, Scorpio, Pisces, Libra, Taurus
Beets	3rd (4th)	Cancer, Scorpio, Pisces, Libra, Capricorn
Berries	3rd (4th)	Cancer, Scorpio, Pisces
Biennials	3rd (4th)	Cancer, Scorpio, Pisces
Broccoli	1st (2nd)	Cancer, Scorpio, Pisces, Libra
Brussels Sprouts	1st (2nd)	Cancer, Scorpio, Pisces, Libra
Bulbs	3rd (4th)	Cancer, Scorpio, Pisces, Taurus, Capricorn
Bulbs (for seed)	2nd	Cancer, Scorpio, Pisces, Taurus, Capricorn
Cabbage	1st (2nd)	Cancer, Scorpio, Pisces, Taurus, Libra
Cantaloupes	2nd (1st)	Cancer, Scorpio, Pisces, Libra
Carrots	3rd	Cancer, Scorpio, Pisces, Libra
Cauliflower	1st (2nd)	Cancer, Scorpio, Pisces, Taurus, Libra
Celery	1st (2nd)	Cancer, Scorpio, Pisces, Taurus
Cereal Grains	1st (2nd)	Cancer, Scorpio, Pisces, Libra
Chard	1st (2nd)	Cancer, Scorpio, Pisces, Taurus, Libra
Corn	1st (2nd)	Cancer, Scorpio, Pisces
Corn (field)	1st (2nd)	Cancer, Scorpio, Pisces, Libra
Cucumbers	1st (2nd)	Cancer, Scorpio, Pisces, Taurus

Eggplant	2nd (1st)	Cancer, Scorpio, Pisces, Taurus, Libra
Garlic	3rd (4th)	Cancer, Scorpio, Pisces, Libra
Hay	1st (2nd)	Cancer, Scorpio, Pisces, Libra
Lettuce	1st (2nd	Cancer, Scorpio, Pisces, Taurus, Libra
Melons	2nd (1st)	Cancer, Scorpio, Pisces
Okra	2nd (1st)	Cancer, Scorpio, Pisces, Taurus, Libra
Onions	3rd (4th)	Cancer, Scorpio, Pisces, Taurus, Libra
Parsley	1st (2nd)	Cancer, Scorpio, Pisces, Libra, Taurus
Peas	2nd (1st)	Cancer, Scorpio, Pisces, Taurus, Libra
Peppers	2nd (1st)	Scorpio, Taurus, Libra, Cancer, Pisces
Perennials	3rd	Cancer, Scorpio, Pisces, Taurus, Capricorn, Libra
Potatoes	3rd (4th)	Cancer, Scorpio, Pisces, Taurus, Libra, Capricorn
Pumpkin	2nd (1st)	Scorpio, Taurus, Libra, Cancer
Radishes	3rd (4th)	Scorpio, Pisces, Taurus, Libra
Rhubarb	3rd	Cancer, Scorpio, Pisces, Taurus
Spinach	1st (2nd)	Cancer, Scorpio, Pisces, Taurus, Libra, Capricorn
Squash	2nd (1st)	Cancer, Scorpio, Pisces, Taurus, Libra, Capricorn
Strawberries (perennial)	3rd (4th)	Cancer, Scorpio, Pisces, Taurus, Libra, Capricorn
Tomatoes	2nd (1st)	Cancer, Scorpio, Pisces, Taurus
Turnips	3rd (4th)	Cancer, Scorpio, Pisces, Taurus, Capricorn

( ) denotes 2nd choice

19

Chapter 3

Transplanting

THE RULE: As outlined in Chapter 2, do your transplanting in the 1st or 2nd Quarter for crops that produce their yield above-ground and in the 3rd or 4th Quarter for those producing below ground, and, in either case, in one of the fruitful or semi-fruitful signs.

In the past, gardening was primarily for self-sufficiency; people grew their own plants. They could control the planting of their seedbeds by the Moon phase and sign. Now, a garden is more often less of a necessity. It can be anything from a hobby to a budget booster. Most people do not make their own seedbeds; they buy plants. Every garden shop in every city or town offers plants for sale.

There is risk here. These seedlings may actually have been planted under adverse conditions. The buyer has no way of knowing the Moon phase or sign under which the seedbed was prepared. Your "hothouse" plants, therefore, may not have all the qualities you might desire, nor may they necessarily possess the qualities you could have achieved had you planted your own seedbed.

But let's be practical. For smaller gardens, a seedbed is not the best approach, or even a desirable one. The garden space you have available may only allow for three or four tomato plants. But even if it were large enough for dozens, would a seedbed be advisable? Probably not. One packet of seeds, one small seedbed, will produce forty or fifty healthy plants. Unless you are going to be "Good Neighbor Sam," supplying plants to all of the gardeners in your immediate area, you are going to be wasting seed, time and effort – and in the end, wasting healthy plants that you can't use or give away.

So, whether you grow your own plants or buy them – and more especially if you buy them – when you are ready to plant them in the soil of your own garden, by all means choose a good phase of the Moon and a fruitful sign.

You can readily see why this is all the more important for those plants that you buy, because you have not been able to control the time they were put into the seedbed, neither the Moon phase nor the sign. Accordingly, they are going to need all the help you can give them so take the time to choose a good Moon phase and a suitable sign. Give them every chance to produce.

No doubt you have already read the chapter on Planting, so there is no need for a complete outline of the Moon's phases, but a quick review might be helpful.

Use the 1st Quarter (New Moon) for transplanting anything that produces above ground, with seeds outside the fruit; use the 2nd Quarter for transplanting anything that produces above the ground, with seeds inside the fruit; use the 3rd Quarter (Full Moon) for transplanting anything that produces in the ground, such as potatoes (both sweet and Irish are now available as plants), or for onion bottoms, not for the green tops. The 4th Quarter is the same as the 3rd Quarter, but use this quarter only when it can't be avoided, because the Moon is losing some of its pizzazz, especially in the last few days of the quarter.

Now, a quick review of the Moon's signs. Since The Rule merely says in a "fruitful or semi-fruitful sign," we should enlarge on that.

With fruitful signs, Cancer is always at the top of the pecking order. Cancer is the nurturer, the symbol of the mothers of the world. Next would be Scorpio and then Pisces. All three are fruitful, water signs, and all three are excellent for transplanting.

When circumstances will not permit transplanting in both a correct phase of the Moon AND in one of these three fruitful water signs, all is not lost. Turn to the semi-fruitful signs – the earth signs, Taurus or Capricorn. Or, you may use the other semi-fruitful sign, Libra, especially good for flowers.

The fruitful and semi-fruitful signs have been listed in the order of strength as far as fruitfulness is concerned, but some signs are better than others for specific things. Tomatoes, for example, do well when transplanted in Cancer. And, as with planting the tomato seed, the 2nd Quarter of the Moon is better than the 1st.

Why do we recommend both Cancer and the 2nd Quarter of the Moon for tomatoes, either from seed or when transplanting? Cancer is a moist, water sign, and it rules, among other things: bottles, breasts, cisterns, canals – anything that will hold water, that will hold liquids, such as veins, arteries, tubs and buckets.

Tomatoes are a watery vegetable (or fruit, or even berry, if you prefer), encased in a container which is the skin and the outer pulp of the fruit. So, you have a natural affinity. The same thing would tend to be true of any other fruit or vegetable that tends to be pulpy or watery. If they produce seeds on the inside, and tend to be a "container," holding together their watery interior, transplanting in Cancer in the 2nd Quarter is the right way to go.

We chose the 2nd Quarter because the tomato is a fruit or vegetable that produces seeds inside rather than outside, such as broccoli.

If you have only skimmed Chapter 2 (Planting), please go back and reread it. It is truly the foundation for all planting, either from seed or seedling, and deals thoroughly with basics.

Another reason for choosing the best possible Moon phase and sign for transplanting is that even though your seedlings may have been planted under adverse aspects, they are now being given a second chance. When you find the best possible conditions for transplanting, the best possible phase of the Moon and the best possible sign, you are greatly enhancing that new beginning.

If you find you simply cannot transplant with both factors (phase and sign) at the optimum, then elect to transplant in a fruitful sign rather than in the correct phase of the Moon. At all costs, you must avoid transplanting in a barren sign. Your aim in gardening is to produce, and a barren sign will simply retard the process. In case you have forgotten, the barren signs are, in order of declining potency: Leo, Gemini, Virgo, Aquarius, Sagittarius and Aries.

Up to this point we have been talking about transplanting from the hothouse or your seedbed to your garden. Such things as pepper, tomato, and even squash and okra plants are now found in garden centers and hardware stores. But what about other types of transplanting: trees, berry bushes, shrubs? These are things that are often transplanted, so let us give them consideration.

As we've stressed, do *all* transplanting in a fruitful sign, including trees, bushes and shrubs. And, as we have pointed out, some fruitful signs are better than others for specific things. We prefer Scorpio for fruit trees, for example, because it will produce a sturdy tree, needed to support the yield. If it were a shrub, we might think first of Pisces, to promote a good, strong root system.

When time is not a factor, you can easily choose the right sign and the right Moon phase for transplanting, but we live in the real world. Gardening has to be fitted in as best you can. So, let us look to the realities.

To enjoy gardening, with the time available, don't let the minor variations in the fruitful signs loom too large in your mind. If the choice is between a good sign and a good phase, the sign is much more important. Remember, any fruitful or semi-fruitful sign will do. That gives you Cancer, Scorpio, Pisces, Taurus and Capricorn. If beauty is a factor, as in an ornamental or a flowering plant, think of Libra. It's not the greatest sign for production, but it's marvelous for beauty.

The point: Whatever your time schedule, there will be a fruitful sign available in a good phase of the Moon. There will never be a quarter phase of the Moon without at least one fruitful or semi-fruitful sign available.

There are people who contend that the correct Moon phase and sign are not important for transplanting, but we disagree. We think it's even more important for you to have – as a minimum – a fruitful sign. This is a new beginning for the plant, a second chance, and if the best possible conditions are made available, then it has an opportunity to overcome, or at least mitigate, earlier debilitating factors it might have had when it was originally planted in the seedbed.

If you are serious about the abundance of your garden, transplanting can't be one of those "when-I-get-the-time" things. It is important. It is on a par with seed planting.

Chapter 4

Companion Planting

To this point, at the beginning of each chapter or each chapter sub-section, you have seen The Rule. There will be no rule in this chapter, because Companion Planting does not, in itself, fall into any Moon phase or Moon sign category.

Are you wondering, therefore, why this chapter is in the book? When good plant companions are together, they protect each other; each will add to the vigor of the other, or to the flavor of the fruit or vegetable produced.

But the reason for including Companion Planting is more basic, more important, more life-giving than that: In selective planting you eliminate, or at least cut down on, poisons used in the garden.

Whether we like it or not, poisons are being introduced into our food supply through many sources: in the seedbed, through the growing and harvesting processes; in storage, whether canned or frozen; and, even in the kitchen.

Now, before you protest too much, do you use aluminum pots and pans? Do certain foods react on those pots and pans, darkening them or brightening them? It happens. You've seen it many times. The acid in the tomato eats into the aluminum, so when you eat the spaghetti sauce you ingest it. If you boil eggs in aluminum, the container turns dark inside. Can this be good for you?

You can argue that aluminum, or aluminum in combination with other ingredients, is used in medicine. It's prescribed by doctors. A valid point. So is this: Many poisons are also medications. Your doctor is trained to dispense poisons. But should you? As you cook, are you really capable of saying how much aluminum in your system is too much? Think about it. To complicate it further, acid is not the only

24

thing that breaks down aluminum; alkalies can do it. So, yes, even in your kitchen you may be adding to the poisons in your body – from your food supply and from your everyday life. The aluminum pot is just one example.

The Federal Food and Drug Administration is not going to protect us from all of this. That would be an impossible task. The Environmental Protection Agency can't do it. As a matter of fact, if you are expecting your government to protect you, you are shirking your own responsibility. It's dangerous to think that the government can – or should – do this job for you. We've all become so bedazzled by the politicians' cradle-to-the-grave siren's song that we're becoming incapable of acting for ourselves.

We must start protecting ourselves, in our kitchens *and* in our gardens. But this book should not be concerned with the kitchen, the bedroom or the bath. It should concentrate on keeping poisons out of the food supply and keeping nutrition high at the source: your garden.

Do you think we are taking this circuitous route to keep from answering the original question: "Why is there a chapter in this book called Companion Planting?"

Here's the answer: When you plant using the phases of the Moon and the signs it passes through in its 28-day-plus cycle, you are planting by (or with) *affinities that occur in nature*. You are simply taking advantage of the natural time the seed has an affinity to the available moisture, when that moisture can be assimilated most effectively.

In addition to tides, the Moon affects all fluids, even those in our body. You are looking for that part of the cycle of the Moon that is most likely to help you achieve the results you have in mind.

Yes, there is a great deal of talk in this book about phases of the Moon and its signs, because that's the way we indicate where and when these affinities exist. When the Moon is in the sign of Cancer, for example, we have a moist and fruitful period, ideal for planting a seed to germinate quickly. This is an affinity occurring in nature, just as dill planted near cabbage will improve the flavor of the cabbage, or just as geraniums planted around or near your roses will help drive off Japanese beetles. We are looking for affinities or antipathies, depending on the end result we wish to accomplish. We want to bring plants together in a way that will allow them to support each other, or in a way that will repel the plant's natural enemies.

Yes, you can control with chemical sprays and dusts – with a myriad of poisons – but you are adding to the problems of your own immune system. You are also killing some of the natural predators that prey on the very insect you are seeking to destroy. And how safe are you when you apply these poisons? How safe is it to eat the foods that have been doused with them? Even when you wash the vegetables thoroughly, are you sure there is no chemical residue on the skin or in the flesh of that fruit?

Throughout this book we have been looking to the Moon's phases and signs for natural affinities or antipathies. Companion planting is a search for the same thing: the natural way to healthful living through nature's abundant combinations of good companions, or nature's own brand of insect repellent.

So let us proceed. We have prepared two charts for this chapter. You can see at a glance those plants that go well with each other and those that definitely do not.

The first of those, Good Companions, shows plants that tend to support each other. (See Good Companions chart at the end of this chapter.)

Just as we have a preference for our neighbors, plants have a very definite preference for their near "neighbors." They support each other. These are the natural affinities we talked about earlier. Planting good companions together offers you an advantage, just as a good Moon phase or sign is an advantage.

Bad Companions (see chart at the end of this chapter), is simply a list of those plants that do not make good neighbors, that have a negative effect on each other. Keep them apart in your garden.

Many of you have seen examples of companion planting all through your lives, even though you may have been unaware of it. In the fall, as you drive through the countryside, you see fields of corn interspersed with bright orange pumpkins, or you see corn in shocks with pumpkins around them. This is companion planting. Corn and pumpkins make excellent neighbors. They contribute to each other. They stimulate each other. Farmers, be assured, do not plant corn and pumpkins just because it's picturesque. They are too practical for that. They are deliberately planting two vegetables that are good companions, good neighbors.

It's a pity, but gardens have changed over the years. Vegetables are planted in a plot behind the fence and the flowers closer to the house. But do you remember your grandmother's garden? It was not just a vegetable patch; it was a beautiful place with flowers and herbs planted all over it. It was a feast for the eyes and, on occasion, the nose, with the smell of mint and marigolds. Was grandmother doing this because she had an eye for beauty? If so, it was only a secondary consideration. No, she planted her flowers and herbs with a purpose. She didn't have a Garden Shoppe to run to for some kind of chemical spray to repel the bugs, mites or aphids she found on her plants. She had something better: she had knowledge of which plants made good neighbors and which ones did not. She knew which plants could help repel the natural enemies of her garden.

Truly, the reasons for her beautiful garden were practical, even though the effect was beautiful, just as the shocks of corn and bright orange pumpkins created what we consider real rural charm.

In your grandmother's garden, for example, you may have seen clumps of garlic planted here and there, at what may have appeared to be random locations throughout. That's because grandmother knew that this aromatic plant was pretty to see, useful in cooking and canning, and, most important, a good repellent for many harmful garden pests. Also, before the days of rampant spraying, garlic was often grown under the trees in the orchard, to protect the fruit.

Marigolds, too, were often spot-planted throughout the garden, as well as at specific locations for specific reasons. She would put a couple of marigolds here and there, because she knew their pungent smell would help keep the pests under control. Marigolds will be all but ignored by the bees visiting your garden, and by the ladybugs, the mantises and other insect predators.

Grandma knew that lemon balm, tarragon, thyme, mint and valerian were also excellent for spot planting all over the garden. She had a very human fear of snakes (even though snakes are insect and mice eaters) so she planted gourds on the garden fence. "Snakes," she said, "don't like the smell of gourd vines."

Chemical sprays and dusts are poisons. They are for killing, make no mistake about that. They are effective, but they decimate the good with the bad. They kill predators that eat the aphids you want to eliminate, and they kill bees that pollinate. This is no place to moralize, but keep this in mind: You need pollination in your garden or it won't produce. Most of the pollination is done by the bees and other insects as they move from blossom to blossom.

We remember visiting a man in Florida a few years ago who always had a productive garden. When we arrived his wife said, "Go on back; he's back there working. Just follow the path."

He was there, on his knees, hand-pollinating squash – a painstaking and tedious job. He had a Q-tip, moving it from flower to flower. We asked why. "No bees," was the answer. "If I didn't do it this way, I'd have no squash and very little of anything else."

The moral: Keep poisons at a minimum by companion planting. Use the natural enemies of the pests who invade your garden.

Some gardeners think half the fun of a garden is the seed catalogues they receive during the snow and ice of January. It is, but we think the planning – the layout – of the garden is also a great deal of fun. We do it on graph paper, with the plans of last year's garden close at hand. Because of blight, we move tomatoes and potatoes each year, being careful they are neither in a spot where either grew the preceding year. This decreases the chance of blight to both crops, thus reducing the need for poisons.

We try to plan the area so that good companions will be side-by-side, and good natural repellents will also be nearby. As you know, tomato plants have a very pungent smell. Cabbage moths know this, too, so they avoid the vicinity of tomatoes. For this reason, one of our choices is to plant tomatoes and cabbages close together. If cabbage moths avoid the area, they will lay no eggs and we will have no cabbage worms.

It is not easy to plan a garden so that all plants are adjacent to good neighbors, but that's where the fun comes in. It's a challenge, a puzzle to be worked out, and it is even more fun if you keep records of your results. Gardening should be a joy from the receipt of the first catalogue right on through to the harvest. And, by working with nature rather than against it, you add to the success of it. Don't we all enjoy succeeding?

While it is true that the bulk of the control of garden pests of all kinds will be in another chapter, there has been, of necessity, some overlapping because companion planting resurrects the good neighbor policy, whether it be for support, for additional strength, for flavor or for pest control. Forgive us, please, for any redundancy.

Chart 2 – Good Companions

Name	Good Companions
Asparagus	Sunflower, Cucumber, Cabbage, Potato, Celery, Tomato, Corn, Cauliflower, Beet, Carrot
Basil	Most garden plants
Beans (Bush)	Potato, Cucumber, Beet, Carrot, Cabbage, Cauliflower, Corn, Savory, Strawberries, Marigolds, Catnip, Nasturtium, Rosemary, Petunia
Beans (Pole)	Potato, Corn, Radish, Marigold, Petunia, Rosemary, Nasturtium
Beets	Onions, Beans, Cabbage, Broccoli, Chard, Brussels Sprouts, Cauliflower, Kohlrabi
Broccoli	Beets, Tomato, Onions, Dill, Sage, Celery, Potato, Mint, Carrot, Rosemary, Thyme, Camomile, Hyssop, Marigold
Cabbage	Same as Broccoli
Cantaloupe	Corn
Carrot	Lettuce, Peas, Cabbage family, Leeks, Onions, Chives, Radishes, Sage, Rosemary
Cauliflower	Same as Broccoli
Celery	Beans, Tomato, Cabbage, Leeks
Chives	Tomato, Carrot, Peas, Grapes, Berries, Apples, Roses
Corn	Potato, Beans, Peas, Melon, Cucumber, Soybean, Pumpkin
Cucumber	Radishes, Corn, Potato, Cabbage, Beans, Sunflower
Dill	Cabbage, Cucumber, Broccoli, Cauliflower, Onions, Lettuce
Eggplant	Tomato, Beans, Potato, Pepper
Garlic	Tomato, Cabbage, Raspberry, Blackberry, Fruit Trees, Roses
Grapes	Hyssop
Henbit	A good general insect repellent for anywhere in the garden, as are Basil, Marigold, Marjoram, Oregano, Tarragon, Mint and Thyme.

Name	Good Companion
Kale	The Cabbage family, Rosemary, Mint, Marigolds, Nasturtium
Kohlrabi	Beet, Onion, Dill, Sage, Celery, Potato, Carrot, Rosemary, Mint, Thyme, Marigold
Lettuce	Strawberries, Carrot, Radish, Tomato, Beet
Marigold	Plant throughout the garden
Mustard	Peas, Beans, Grapes, Fruit Trees
Onions	Beets, Carrot, Tomato, Lettuce, Camomile, Savory, the Cabbage family
Parsley	Tomato, Pepper, Corn, Roses
Peas	Radishes, Carrots, Corn, Cucumber, Potato, Beans, Squash, Turnips
Pepper	Tomato, Beans, Eggplant, Onion, Carrot, Basil, Parsley
Potato	Beans, the Cabbage family, Corn, Peas, Eggplant, Squash, Basil, Horse Radish, Marigold
Pumpkin	Corn
Radishes	Chervil, Peas, Lettuce, Cucumber, Melons, Nasturtium and other root crops
Raspberries	Garlic
Rutabagas	Peas
Sage	Carrots, Tomato, the Cabbage family, Rosemary
Spinach	Strawberries, Eggplant, Celery, Cauliflower
Squash	Corn, Borage
Strawberries	Borage, Bush Beans, Spinach, Lettuce
Sunflower	Cucumber, Pumpkin, Squash
Swiss Chard	Beans, Onions, Kohlrabi
Tomatoes	Asparagus, Cucumber, the Cabbage family, Lettuce, Onions, Mustard, Carrot, Basil, Borage, Parsley, Sage, Mint, Rosemary, Marigold
Turnip	Peas

Chart 3 – Bad Companions

Name	Bad Companions
Basil	Rue
Beans (Bush)	Onions, Garlic, Shallots, Leeks, Fennel
Beans (Pole)	Beets, Onions, Leeks, Shallots, Kohlrabi, Chard, Kale
Beets	Mustard, Pole Beans
Broccoli	Strawberries, Lettuce
Cabbage	Strawberries, Lettuce
Cantaloupe	None
Carrots	Dill
Cauliflower	Strawberries, Lettuce
Chives	None
Corn	None
Cucumbers	Potatoes, Sage
Dill	Carrots
Eggplant	None
Fennel	Most plants in the garden. Plant fennel outside the garden, but especially never near pole beans or kohlrabi.
Garlic	Peas, Beans
Kale	Pole Beans, Strawberries
Kohlrabi	Tomatoes, Pole Beans, Fennel
Lettuce	Keep away from the entire cabbage family.
Mustard	Beets
Onions	Beans, Peas
Parsley	None
Parsnips	None
Peas	Garlic, Onions, Leeks, Shallots, Leeks
Peppers	Kohlrabi, Fennel
Potatoes	Tomatoes, Pumpkin, Sunflower, Apple, Cherry, Raspberry, Walnuts, Cucumbers

Name	Bad Companion
Radishes	Hyssop
Rutabagas	Mustard
Sage	Cucumbers
Spinach	None
Strawberries	The entire cabbage family
Sunflower	Potato
Swiss Chard	Pole Beans
Tomatoes	Potatoes, Kohlrabi, Fennel
Turnips	Mustard

Chapter 5

Pruning

This chapter will be made up of two sections: To Encourage
Growth and To Discourage Growth, both of which are valid purposes
for pruning.

To Encourage Growth

THE RULE: Always prune in the 3rd or 4th Quarter of the Moon
and in one of the fruitful signs, especially if you are pruning a producer
rather than an ornamental.

All plants benefit from pruning. Sometimes it's for the removal of
suckers so the plant can send its strength to the fruit-bearing branches;
sometimes it's simply shaping the plant or tree for beautification; and,
sometimes it's to open the top of the plant or tree to let sunlight in for
healthy production of fruit. These are a few of the reasons for pruning.
There are many, and we do not intend to cover them all.

The point we want to make is that pruning is a vital part of gardening or orchard care. Don't neglect it. Prune to encourage growth or to
control it; prune dead limbs or limbs that cross each other, scrubbing
off bark and inviting disease; prune for larger fruit or for a larger flower; prune to prevent the interior of a tree from becoming too dense,
shutting out sunlight; or, prune to achieve a preconceived shape.

If you have inherited a problem – let's say you have just bought an
old farm and you find the orchard has been neglected – then pruning
becomes an absolute necessity, not just for maintenance or beauty, but
for production. In the case of neglect, all the pruning that needs to be
done may not be possible at one time, or in one season. Radical pruning could prove too much for the neglected tree. Proper pruning will
take time. Go about it with an over-all plan. Do only what is needed for

the health of the tree, and, ultimately, for production. Know the nature of the shrub; know what can and should be pruned. Pruning, in some instances, can be final. This will differ with each tree or shrub, of course, so if you are in doubt, contact your county agent or send for information from your state agricultural agency.

Without advice from anyone and without regard to the nature of the tree or shrub, you can begin to prune the dead branches or any diseased wood. A neglected tree can be overgrown, with criss-crossing branches that block sunlight or create abrasions where parasites can enter. Prune to eliminate these conditions.

For best fruit production, sunlight must reach all parts of the tree. If the crown is too thick, sunlight is diffused or blocked. For years, peach trees have had radical trimming of the crown, allowing plenty of sunlight to reach all parts of the spread branches. Recently, apple trees are being pruned using a similar technique.

Now, let us amplify The Rule stated at the beginning of this chapter: Pruning should be done in either the 3rd or 4th Quarter of the Moon. The reason is quite simple: This is a time of declining energy, declining growth and, therefore, pruning will affect the shrub or tree less deleteriously. And, while we are speaking of periods of declining energy, let us talk about those wintertime periods when the sap is down and the tree – from a growth point of view – is all but asleep. This is an excellent time for pruning, because it utilizes the low energies of the tree. Because of the lack of sap in the branches, "bleeding" will be less, and healing will be faster.

There is a second reason why pruning a producing tree is best done in winter. It is dormant in cold weather; it is in a state of "suspension." In the spring, when the sap begins to rise, the tree "comes to life." During this period, as the sap is coming up, the buds are set for the coming fruit crop. If you delay pruning until after this bud-setting process has begun, new growth will form, but it will be smaller, tenderer and thus subject to damage by the first late spring cold weather or by a light frost.

In the long run, pruning is good for your tree, but it does produce shock. Your job is to lessen that shock. What you are doing is surgery, and while surgery is often necessary and beneficial, it is still a shock to the human or plant system. Use the periods of low energy, when the sap is down, preferably when the Moon is in the 3rd or 4th Quarter.

So much for the phases of the Moon mentioned in The Rule at the beginning of this chapter. We will now consider the rest of it: "... in one of the fruitful signs."

At this point, as you read Chapter 5, you are becoming familiar with the fruitful and semi-fruitful signs. There are six choices: Cancer, Scorpio and Pisces (fruitful), and Taurus, Capricorn and Libra (semi-fruitful). Any of these signs are suitable for pruning to encourage growth, but each has a quality not entirely possessed by the other; and each, therefore, can work better with specific plants or trees, depending on the purpose for the pruning.

What is your aim? Is it beauty? Is this an ornamental? If so, by all means use Libra. Is it a fruit tree where both sturdiness and good fruit are the primary objectives? If so, use Scorpio, or even Taurus. If you are looking to encourage root growth, then perhaps you will opt for Pisces. Cancer might well be the choice if production is the only aim. The first choice for pruning, we think, is Scorpio.

As we talked to people about sign gardening, we heard some un-orthodox ideas expressed. When such a thing occurs only once or twice, we pay little attention to it, but when we hear it on several different occasions, and in widely separated areas, we think it should at least be mentioned. Here is one of those: If you are having trouble keeping birds out of the grapes or if you are troubled by worm infestations, prune just before the Full Moon (late 2nd Quarter), and in the sign of Scorpio, if possible. If this is not possible, use Taurus or Cancer, in that order.

Here is still another variation from The Rule: If you prune trees or vines – especially the heavier bleeders – in the 3rd or 4th Quarter and in the sign of Capricorn, you will prevent both bleeding and infected or damaged prune sites. This idea does not vary from The Rule in phase, and it does utilize a semi-fruitful sign. Why Capricorn? Could it be because Cancer, Scorpio and Pisces are all water signs and might, therefore, encourage bleeding? If so, we can at least comprehend why Capricorn would be preferred over these three, and even over Taurus, which tends more to moisture than dry Capricorn. This theory, this variation has validity. Capricorn could be a good choice for bleeders.

This next example, however, just doesn't fit in at all. Some people say they like to prune grape vines in Sagittarius, but we do not recommend it, nor any other fire sign. You prune only when there is need, and you do it when it will do the least possible harm. Grapes not only need but require pruning, because the fruit, as with roses, grows only on new wood. Pruning, therefore, is essential for good crops, but it should be done with the least possible shock to the vine.

Some people feel pruning on a growing Moon (1st or 2nd Quarter) will stimulate growth in an established tree or plant. Try this if you like, but we prefer The Rule as stated at the beginning of the chapter. Our reason: the prune site is a wound, no matter how necessary it may be. And, because it is a wound, we would prefer to inflict it at a time when the tree or shrub is most able to handle the shock. That would be, of course, in the 3rd or 4th Quarter of the Moon, when energies are declining. This would give the wound healing time before the rising energies of the New Moon begin to affect it.

Prune about a quarter of an inch above a bud and choose one that is pointing outward. New growth will start from this bud, so don't choose a bud that will send a new branch back into the interior of the tree. All pruning need not be done when the sap is down, but in any case, you should wait until after harvest – after the tree is out of production.

When you think of pruning you may think of "loppers" and a saw, or even of hand clippers, but all pruning is not done in this manner. You can prune a plant in many ways. Pinching is a type of pruning. Some ornamentals will produce profusely if they are not permitted to go to seed. Marigolds are one example. Pinching or pruning is necessary to prevent this. It can be done during the growing cycle, if required, but prevent shock by utilizing the 3rd or 4th Quarter of the Moon in a fruitful sign.

Pruning or pinching removes unwanted growth. It allows strength to go where it is needed. In addition, if you have a profusion of buds, pinching half of them can reward you with larger and healthier flowers.

As you prune, try to follow the general lines of the plant. This will encourage natural growth and shape. Nature sometimes – even quite often – produces too much. This is her way of keeping the strain alive. But profusion may not be a part of your over-all scheme and you must pinch, clip or snip. Strive to produce a plant shaped to your liking and a garden growth according to your personal plan.

Another reason for removing some of the natural abundance of nature is to prevent damage. Too many blossoms will produce too much fruit, which could prove to be too heavy for the branch. The resulting break is another place for disease to strike.

A quick review: To encourage growth, always prune in a decreasing Moon, 3rd or 4th Quarter, and choose one of the six fruitful or semi-fruitful signs, depending on your time availability for the chore and the results you wish to achieve.

To Discourage Growth

THE RULE: Always prune in the 1st or 2nd Quarter of the Moon and in one of the less potent barren signs, with Aries or Sagittarius recommended.

As usual, we will look at the Moon phases first. The 1st or 2nd Quarter is chosen because it represents a time of the Moon's growth, from the New Moon until the Full Moon. We are actively seeking this energy because we want it to help the retardation of growth. We do not want to destroy the tree or the plant or shrub, so we are using this energy with the weakest of the barren signs — with the least destructive of them — because our purpose is to retard, not to destroy.

In order of their potency, Leo heads the list. Leo would most certainly destroy if used in a growing phase of the Moon. The same would be true of Gemini (the twins) and Virgo (the virgin). These are signs for destroying, not for retarding or discouraging. Aquarius is the next most powerful of the barren signs, followed by Sagittarius and Aries.

In recommending signs for the discouraging of growth we have gone to the least potent end of the scale. Our recommendation begins with Aries and then Sagittarius. You could use Aquarius, but only as a last resort.

This combination, a weak barren sign and a strong phase of the Moon, will bring about negative action, and that is what we are looking for. We want to negate the growing process, to discourage it, to retard it. We are not looking to bring it to a complete halt, as might be our desire when we are trying to clear our garden of briars, young locust trees or other outcroppings.

Now, when you are pruning, even if the desired result is to discourage growth, you still are trying to bring about many of the same things being achieved when you prune to encourage growth: You are still trying to shape the tree or shrub; you are still trying to eliminate abrading branches; you are still trying to keep it a living, growing thing. For these reasons, a review of the beginning of this chapter might be in order. Some of it is sure to be applicable.

Pruning is not just branch removal, although that tends to be the first thought the word evokes. Pruning is also, for example, suckering, which we advise for corn or tomatoes. A sucker is a subordinate shoot from the bud, the stem, or the root of a plant. It is an unwanted appendage that should be removed or it will sap strength from the main plant or tree, thus reducing the harvest. This kind of removal – suckering being only one kind – is also a kind of pruning and follows The Rule for discouraging unwanted growth.

There you have it, the two reasons for pruning and the two rules that apply. Each one, as to phase, is a complete reversal of the other. That is because the two aims are exactly opposite. One is to encourage and the other to discourage.

Chapter 6

Destroying
Unwanted Growth

THE RULE: Destroy in the 3rd or 4th Quarter of the Moon, in one of the barren signs: Leo, Gemini or Virgo preferred. Exception: Destroy unwanted watery or pulpy plants in the 1st or 2nd Quarter, but only in the sign of Leo.

First, the phases of the Moon. For most unwanted growth, the waning Moon is recommended, with a preference for the 4th Quarter when the Moon's energies are at the lowest ebb. The later this work can be done in the dying phase of the Moon the better. This will permit the barren sign used in the destruction to operate at its highest capacity.

The one exception to the phase part of The Rule is when you seek to destroy watery or pulpy plants – wild onions being one example, or wild grape vines. With this exception you must use the sign of the heart, Leo, and a growing Moon is recommended because the energies of the Moon will increase the bleeding process. This method can be used with any pulpy plant that tends to bleed when cut or bruised.

Our first thought of a pulpy pest is always wild onions. If you have had experience with them, you know how persistent they can be. In a pasture they can really cause havoc because milk is affected when a cow eats this pungent weed.

They are a persistent pest and difficult to eradicate, so try cutting them when the Moon is in Leo, after the New Moon. You will be pleased with the results. The barren quality of Leo, its faculty for causing bleeding, combined with the action of a waxing Moon, will eliminate this pest as no other phase and sign combination can do.

But, keep in mind, this is the exception, and it applies only to watery, pulpy plants, with the Moon in the sign of the heart: Leo.

In this discussion of the barren signs, we will give a thumbnail description of each, and then a more detailed explanation of the reasons for the barren quality. Then, we will cite the special uses for each of the signs.

When destroying watery or pulpy plants, it may not be possible to use Leo in the 1st or 2nd Quarter. If so, the 3rd quarter might be used. If this is not possible, then Leo is still recommended in whatever quarter phase is available. Leo surpasses all other barrens signs for inducing bleeding, which makes it ideal for any plant that weeps readily at a cut or bruise site.

Barren Signs

1. Leo – the lion – ruling the heart. Never plant in Leo. Use this sign for destruction purposes.

2. Gemini – the twins – ruling the arms (and lungs). The second most destructive sign.

3. Virgo – the virgin – ruling the bowels. The only feminine sign that is completely barren.

4. Aquarius – the waterbearer – ruling the ankles and lower legs. Better for destroying than Sagittarius which follows, but only slightly better.

5. Sagittarius – the archer – ruling the thighs.

6. Aries – the ram – ruling the head. The least powerful barren sign.

In destroying, you have two considerations to make: The phase of the Moon and the sign. Generally, the last quarter (4th) is best for destruction, but, as we indicated earlier in this chapter, there are some situations that could respond better to another phase of the Moon.

Look at the six signs listed above. Five of them are masculine. The one exception is Virgo, the virgin. By the very term, she is the mother of nothing; she is not a producer. The masculine signs, as with the masculine gender, cannot give birth and are, therefore, in this sense of the word, barren. Virgo is, and will remain, a virgin: So she is, by this measure, barren.

The explanation of how or why each of the six signs don't reproduce is sufficient reason to bar them from use in planting. But does it follow that they are also signs to be used for destruction? We believe so. And for the purpose of destruction some signs are better than others. Let us look at them individually.

Leo – the lion – ruling the heart. First, it's a fire sign, ruled by the

Sun. Fire signs and air signs, masculine signs, are not the nurturers of the world. As stated, Leo is ruled by the Sun which, in turn, rules heat, deserts, exhaustion, fatherhood (not motherhood), fevers, males (not females) and pomp (rather than practicality). These are just a few of the things ruled by the Sun, but you can see that none of them lend themselves to reproduction. Without question, the Moon in Leo is not a sign for planting.

Why is it a sign for destruction? It's because the Sun, the ruler of Leo, has no hint of water about it. Without water all things die. Use this sign to dry the flow of moisture in the plant. Use it (it rules the heart) to cause bleeding at the wound site or to turn the soil so the roots will be exposed to the heat.

Keep this in mind: Plants or vines cut during Leo will be set back severely, or even die. Don't trim ornamentals under this sign.

Fire signs are signs for destroying. Heat destroys. When the Sun is in Leo (roughly July 23 to August 23 of each year), it is a poor time for either planting or transplanting because of the summer heat. This is within the period that is generally considered Dog Days, the hottest days of the year. Because of the heat, this period of time is excellent for destroying unwanted growth. But you need not wait until summer; just choose a time when the Moon is in the sign of Leo and you will get the same effect.

Gemini – the twins – ruling the arms and lungs. Till the soil in this sign to kill roots; weed in this sign to prevent regrowth. Gemini is a mutable air sign. There is no hint of moisture in it. If you wish to slow the growth of your lawn, for example, cut it when the Moon is in the sign of Gemini, and preferably when the Moon is waning (Full Moon or after, but prior to the New Moon).

Do not plant or transplant in Gemini. Do not graft or airlayer. This is a good time for stirring the soil to kill weeds or a good time to pinch buds to prevent unwanted growth. It is also a good sign for the elimination of pests or vermin. If you have a problem with rats or mice, go after them, particularly in the 3rd or 4th Quarter.

Gemini, by most standards, is the second most destructive sign. Accordingly, it is not a good sign for planting, and yet we know of successful gardeners who always wait for the Twins to plant their beans. We know of others who use the Twins for planting cucumbers and melons. We found this a real paradox. Perhaps it's because Gemini is one of the twin or dual signs. Pisces is also a dual sign which happens to be

41

productive, so why not use it instead of Gemini? You may do as you wish with this one, but we prefer to avoid it altogether.

Virgo – the virgin – ruling the bowels. This, like Leo and Gemini, is not a good sign for any kind of planting, transplanting or other methods of propagation. It is an excellent time for any kind of elimination of growth, weeds, trees, bushes, but do not use this sign for the sterilization of animals. There are other suitable signs. This will be fully explained in another chapter.

It is bothersome that Virgo, an earth sign, is not considered productive when the other two are. Taurus is good, Capricorn is fair. We pondered over this point. Is it because the ruler of Virgo is Mercury, a nonsexual or neuter planet? We're not sure, but it could be a reason. Or is it because Virgo rules the bowels, which suggests elimination? That's what destroying is, the elimination of an unwanted plant or animal pest. Nevertheless, we know of people who use this sign for planting flowers. Virgo can produce foliage, so for some leafy flowers – coleus, for example – it may be acceptable, but we don't recommend it.

Virgo is the sign of the virgin – not a producer nor a germinator. We will continue to think of it as the third most potent sign for destroying unwanted growth. Consider it and then use your own judgment.

Aquarius – the waterbearer – ruling the legs. This is another air sign. Keep in mind that air and fire signs are generally poor producers, therefore, represent good times for destroying unwanted growth. The planet ruler of Aquarius is Uranus, ruling: abnormalities, alienation, bachelors (non-producers), debacles, detours, eccentricities, miscarriages (another form of non-production), radiation, rejection and separations. With these few examples, you begin to realize the nature of Uranus, ruler of Aquarius, and you can see why this is a sign for destroying and not for planting or producing.

Sagittarius – the archer – ruling the thighs. Another fire sign. You might think of all fire signs as burners, as destroyers, rather than nurturers. This might be a little unfair to the fire signs, but it does help you to keep in mind that fire signs won't produce, that fire signs should be used to destroy. Jupiter is the ruler of Sagittarius. To give you an idea, Jupiter also rules: abscesses, abundance (overdone), celibacy (non-productive), corpulence (again, something overdone), enlargement, excesses, flabbiness, gluttony, opulence, surpluses, tumors, virgins or virginity (non-productive) and warts.

These are only a few examples, but you can see the nature of

Jupiter's rulership over Sagittarius, and some of the reasons this is a sign for destroying, not for production. Sagittarius, like Aquarius, is generally considered to be barren. If time will not permit planting at some other time, Sagittarius may be slightly better than Aquarius, but, where possible, use these two signs as alternates to Leo, Gemini and Virgo, for destroying unwanted growth or weeds.

Aries – the ram – ruling the head. Here again, another fire sign. This sign is ruled by the planet Mars, which in mythology is the god of war. Is this significant? It could be. It is an interesting point. Look at some of the other things ruled by Mars: abrasions, accidents, arguments, blazes, brimstone, butchers, carnage, cremation, fevers, discord, fires, furnaces, heat, lust, males (non-producers of offspring), opposition, perils, soldiers, warriors (destroyers perhaps?), and wrath. These few examples tend to amplify the destructive qualities of Aries. But it is a far safer sign for planting (or a far less effective sign for destroying) than Leo, Gemini or Virgo.

Many consider Aries a barren sign, but this opinion is not universal. There are people who intentionally use Aries for planting vines, or for anything where rapid growth is desired, or even for planting vegetables or flowers where it is important to have sturdy stalks. Also, because of fast growth and sturdy stalks, there are people who plant in Aries all of the above-the-ground vegetables that have been mentioned earlier. But, of course, the Moon phase, too, must be right – 1st and 2nd Quarters. Aries is the least destructive of the barren signs, so you may use it if you must, if circumstances give you little choice in planting times, or when you are transplanting.

Time can be a problem. There are several choices of ideal or good times in each month for planting or for destroying, but sometimes our daily lives makes the use of these times impossible. When it happens, look for an alternative. Aries could be such an alternative.

Because Aries, and even Sagittarius, are not as virulent as Leo, Gemini and Virgo, these two signs, in combination with the aid of the growing Moon (1st or 2nd Quarter), are used when you seek to simply retard growth.

While we are on the subject of destroying, Virgo is not a good sign for castration or sterilization, nor are Libra and Scorpio. We recommend Taurus, Sagittarius, Capricorn or Pisces. There is a part of this book that specifically deals with castration. See Chapter 10, Elsewhere Around the Homestead.

In this chapter we seem to be stressing the elimination of unwanted plant growth, but the same application may be used when you seek to destroy unwanted animal life, or warts, moles, corns or superfluous hair. Use The Rule for weeds, thistle, poison ivy, fungus growth, insects or pests. We do not recommend poison sprays. But if you ARE using poisons for vermin, mice, rats, dispense it during the 3rd or 4th Quarter with the Moon in Aquarius.

A quick recap: When you wish to destroy growth by weeding, cutting, hoeing, spraying, do so in the signs of Leo, Gemini or Virgo. If these are not available to you, use Aquarius or Sagittarius. Destroying is best done in the dark of the Moon, with the last Quarter being preferable, i.e., the quarter preceding the New Moon. For destroying pulpy, watery plants, utilize the 1st or 2nd Quarter, with the Moon in Leo.

There is one other facet of destroying unwanted growth that should be included in this section. We don't understand – not specifically – how it ties in with the signs of the phases of the Moon, but most people who successfully plant by the signs are aware of these four periods when bushes, shrubs, trees or plants may be eliminated with very little regrowth.

Ember Days. When you are using your almanac or calendar, you will see listed four sets of three entries each marked "Ember Days." Some almanacs only list one Ember Day in each series of three. Only Wednesday will be shown, but the following Friday and Saturday are also Ember Days, even if they are not marked as such.

Even if your calendar or almanac does not list Ember Days, they are reasonably easy to establish. The first set of three: Wednesday, Friday and Saturday, will appear in February or March, depending on the arrival of Easter for that particular year. The second set will vary from year to year, just as the first one did, but it will be found in either May or June. The third set always appears in September, usually near the middle of the month, and the last set is always in mid-December.

If your almanac or calendar does not show Ember Days, the first set of three can be determined this way: Lent begins on Ash Wednesday. The first day of the first set of Ember Days for any year will always fall on the Wednesday of the week following Ash Wednesday. Some prefer to say that Ember Days begin on the Wednesday following the first Sunday in Lent. Either way, the result is the same.

The second set of Ember Days begins on the Wednesday following Whitsunday, or Pentecost.

The third set always begins on the Wednesday after the first Sunday following the festival of the Holy Cross.

The fourth set occurs in mid-December on the first Wednesday following the third Sunday of Advent.

There are four sets of Ember Days, just as there are four seasons, although Ember Days do not fall in any specific slot within the four seasons. Ember Days are religious holidays within the tenets of several different religions, and, as such, are days for prayer and fasting. But these religious holidays – said to be excellent for destroying unwanted growth – do not fall into any Moon phase, or sign. They can occur in any of the four phases of the Moon, and in any sign.

Why are Ember Days mentioned here at all, since they do not specifically tie in with the phases of the Moon or the signs? We elected to cite these periods because they are used by many farmers and gardeners who know the significance of both the Moon sign and phase and who still believe Ember Days are good periods for destroying. Ember Days may have a value for you.

Unwanted growth cut during Ember Days, regardless of the phase of the Moon, will die or come back so weakened that it is an easy matter to eliminate. We have tried this on a hillside with a great many locust trees of various sizes. As you know, locusts spread rapidly from their own root system, and soon you can have a forest of unwanted trees. After several other futile attempts, a neighbor suggested we cut the locusts during the Ember Days that usually precede the Spring Equinox. It worked. There were few remaining locusts the next spring, and they were easy to deal with. That hillside is now a fruit orchard. It was valueless – even an eyesore before that. The only negative aspect here is that when the locusts were gone, the bees were not happy, because locust bloom is a valued honey source. It is considered the Cadillac of honeys in many areas.

Yes, it is true that one drop of water does not make an ocean, so the one-time use of Ember Days doesn't prove it always works, but it did for us, and we have only one hillside that needed this treatment. However, should we ever again need to rid an area of noxious growth, you can bet your life it will be done during Ember Days.

It is also said that the weather can be foretold by Ember Days. Record the weather on the first of those days and that will be the weather, generally speaking, until the arrival of the next set of Ember Days. For example, if the weather on the Ember Day that occurs in December is foul, cold and wet, then expect a bad winter, since the next set of Ember Days will not occur until that period thirty-five to forty days prior to Easter.

Another use that farmers have for Ember Days is to foretell the price their produce or crops will bring for the year. In this instance, the Ember Days of late winter or early spring are the set usually used. If the first Ember Day falls on the 10th of the month, or earlier, prices for all farm products will be low that year. If the first Ember Day falls on the 11th or later, especially the last half of the month, prices will be high.

We garden, we do not farm, so this aspect has never been put to test by us. But we do have neighbors who take Ember Days just as seriously as they do the signs when they plan their activities, whether it be planting or clearing or laying in wood and food.

Chapter 7

Natural Pest Control

THE RULE: Use nature to keep a balance, but if you must have additional help, use repellents rather than poisons.

The reason for avoiding poisons is readily apparent: You are growing your own food supply, and you do not want to introduce poisons into it. Always remember: Your purpose is not to eliminate anything from your garden; all you want to do – or need to do – is control those pests so your own harvest is sufficient.

Above all, your aim should be to help maintain the balance of nature. Poisons may help with an aphid problem, but poisons could also kill your "friends," in the garden who are a part of nature's chain. They eat aphids.

All this, of course, is easier said than done, but it is far from an impossible job. Chart 4, How To Repel Pests, at the end of this chapter, will give you an alphabetical listing of common garden pests and suggestions for natural repellents. These are not poisons. They are flowers or edible plants that certain garden pests find displeasing. The pests will search for another food source, and that is all you are seeking.

Remember, you are not trying to kill; you are trying to control. There is a purpose in nature's over-all scheme for every plant, animal and insect in the universe, as well as man. As a gardener, you're not trying to eradicate any pest or predator, you're only trying to control the area where you make your garden, farm or home.

In addition to planting specifically to control pests, there are some other techniques that may be employed. The onion peels from your kitchen, for example, are excellent for repelling beetles. Scatter some under and around your squash plants. And remember, it is all bio-degradable, so you are enriching your soil at the same time.

In some circumstances, it's best to use the oldest method known: Remove pests by hand.

Slugs, for instance, can be a problem. Trap them or hand-pick them to remove them from your garden. To do this, wet an area where they seem to be, lay a few boards on these damp places and then each morning lift the boards and remove the slugs. It won't be long before you have them under control.

Before the days of heavy spraying for everything, do you remember helping to pick potato bugs off the plants? It was the common method of ridding potatoes of this pest, and it is still a good method today. They are of a size and color that can be seen easily and removed.

Another good technique is spraying with non-poisonous sprays. Try the method your grandmother used: spraying with soapy water. Note the use of the word "soap" here, and not "detergent." Never use a detergent. There are still a few soaps left on your grocery shelves. Fels Naphtha is one. Or, you can make your own soap – real lye soap – and it is the best. The recipe is on the lye can. Try it.

If you're not up to making soap and if you are so "with" the 20th Century that everything must be done for you – prepared and pre-packaged – at least one manufacturer has your needs in mind. There's a safe soap spray on the market. It's sold at many garden supply centers and was developed by Agro-Chem, Inc. If your store doesn't have it, ask them to get it for you.

You can control pests with this soap spray, and you can harvest the vegetables even the day the spraying is done. It's safe for human beings, but it should be washed off the vegetables, of course. It's also biodegradable, so you're not putting something into the soil that will remain there or foul the downstream water supply. Soap spray can be used indoors or outdoors, for aphids, whiteflies, scale insects, spider mites and mealy bugs.

Another natural spray is made of the very pests that are giving you the trouble. Gather a quantity of the offending insects, put them in your blender with water and create your own "insecticide." After you have thoroughly blended the bugs and the water, strain it, so you won't gum up your spray gun. You'll find this spray cheap and effective. It's your version of toxin antitoxin, or "bug against bug," and it works. It will discourage or eliminate those pests, and it will not hurt those insects or bees you want in your garden because of the benefits they bring.

As an example, your problem is an excess of bean beetles. Gather some – handpick them – and then blend thoroughly with water. Strain the mixture, and spray your bean plants. You'll be astonished. Mix only the quantities needed for spraying at one time, however, because the mixture will not keep.

No one method will work with all garden pests. This "blended bug spray" will not work with Japanese beetles, but several baited traps in the garden are usually enough to keep this pest to a workable minimum. Also, if you have trouble with Japanese beetles, the planting of garlic, savory, chives, white geraniums, zinnias or castor beans – alone or in combination – in selected spots around your garden will be a big deterrent. Japanese beetles avoid these plants.

Here's another effective spray, safe for humans and effective. When the population of any specific pest is getting ahead of you, make a spray of a particular plant that repels them. Ground up marigolds in plain water, for example, will be effective against an influx of aphids. Many natural things are offensive to certain of the insect pests. (See Chart 4.) Use them in a water solution for spraying. Onion, garlic, hot peppers and the aromatic herbs are the ones we tend to think of first, but there are others. Chart 4 will give you ideas for specific pests.

Here is something else to consider. It's a relatively new frontier – or at least new to us – but biological sprays are being developed. Selectively-poisonous substances are being derived from naturally-occurring diseases that have an effect on a specific pest. A spray is then made from these selectively-poisonous substances, which will affect that pest and that pest alone.

For example, there is now on the market a biological spray developed specifically for cabbage worms. It does harm other caterpillars, so you might be cutting down on the butterfly population when you spray. Nevertheless, there is such a selective spray sold under the trade names of DiPel and Thuricide. Very likely these sprays are used primarily by large growers of cabbages, but it's a step in the right direction, especially since such a selective spray is for a specific pest and will not harm other, perhaps desirable, insects or the pollinating bees. Birds, too, are safe from such a spray, and so are people.

Then you may hear about "natural sprays," sprays made from plants and roots and are, therefore, natural rather than chemical. They are highly touted because they are safe for human beings and because they are biodegradable, which is to say the poison residue does not remain in the soil long after the spraying is over.

49

Read the label carefully. Maybe they are non-toxic to human beings, maybe they are biodegradable – both highly desired qualities – but will they kill all insects indiscriminately, the bad and the good? And if so, is this really what you are looking to do? Do you want your garden friends to perish with your garden enemies? Remember this: Your friends in the garden, the lady bugs for example, will repopulate much more slowly than your garden enemies. Whether natural or chemical, a poison is a poison.

And, before we leave the subject of so-called natural sprays, there is one other caution that must be made: Some of these naturals will have a botanical base, but the manufacturer may have added "boosters," chemical boosters, to make the spray more effective. *If you buy sprays, be a label reader!*

Still another natural spray is Pyrethrum, made from the daisy. It is safe for humans, according to the manufacturer's test. It has the added advantage of being safe for the gardener's two great friends: bees and ladybugs.

But Pyrethrum is *not* safe for all beneficial insects in your garden. So, if you use it, you will be cutting your own forces, creating an imbalance that will allow some plant-eater or plant-sucker to become stronger because its enemies are gone.

And, too, Pyrethrum kills earthworms – the gardener's best soil-building friend. Our point here is simply this: Pyrethrum is one of the safest sprays for you and your family, and yet it can play havoc with the natural balance of your garden if great care is not used.

The key here is the sparing use of all poisons, whether so-called natural or chemical, because each of them will have side effects that may not be a part of your plan.

Rotenone is another of the so-called natural poisons, but this one IS poisonous to human beings if it comes in contact with the skin. It is also poisonous to humans if it is ingested. Think about it. Can you get all the poison off the tomato before you eat it, or is there still some part of that poison inside? Let's give the devil his due: This is a poison that breaks down into harmless material when exposed to sunlight and air, so the poisons won't stay in the earth and that is a plus. Rotenone will kill many garden pests, but it also kills bees and a host of other beneficial insects.

Still another danger: Rotenone is poisonous to fish, so the runoff from your garden could cause other problems downstream, or in your pond. Think before you use it. It's true that the Sun and the air will break this poison down into harmless matter, so it's a question of how much breakdown occurs before it gets into the water supply.

There are many reasons for a lack of balance in the insect population in your garden. The fault is usually man-made. You might have created an environment unfriendly to your friendly predators, or perhaps your garden is adjacent to a one-crop field that has been heavily sprayed. Try to cultivate your garden "friends" to create an environment that will follow nature's pattern. Such an environment will help to sustain a balance in your garden.

Predators — ladybugs, spiders, toads and even birds — can be affected by poisons. Or, you may be killing off the parasites. Parasites are things you may not have been aware of because they are so small, but they will live in or on another insect, sapping it of its strength, or even killing it. While unseen, these parasites are a real factor in controlling herbivorous (plant-eating) insects. Encourage them, don't kill them with poisons.

If you must spray with a poison, do so selectively and with great care. Without care, you could end up worsening your condition instead of bettering it.

When you kill garden pests with poisons, and at the same time kill all the natural predators in your garden, you open the door to an even larger infestation from within the garden, the yard or an open field of a neighbor. The flood gate has been opened, so to speak, because you have killed off the predators. You have made a safe haven for another wave of the pests you were out to destroy. Without natural enemies, these pests can proliferate. At this point, your task of spraying with poisons becomes a never-ending cycle.

Even with selected poisons, even using the utmost care, such spraying is fraught with danger. There is good reason for this: Plant-eating insects are less likely move about. They move only to hunt food, so they will stay right there on the beans, eggplant or squash until they have made "lace" of your garden.

On the other hand, the predators or the parasites (the good guys) must move about, hunting for prey or a host to attack. And, in moving about, they can move through the area you have poisoned. That could be the end of them. So, inadvertently, you have killed the natural enemies of the pest you meant to control.

Here is another reason why spraying with poisons can do more harm to the predators and parasites than it will do to the pests. Garden pests – the leaf eaters – have a very short reproductive cycle. When you kill them, there is another batch waiting in the wings – another onslaught ready for your garden. But this is not the case with your garden friends – the predators or the parasites – for they then have a much longer reproductive cycle. When they are killed, it takes longer to repopulate the garden in numbers sufficient to help you with pest control.

Because of this difference in reproductive cycles, your garden is likely to have, in actual numbers, fewer friends than it has enemies. This situation is not dissimilar to the growth of weeds as compared with garden vegetables. The cycle for weeds is short, while it may take a season for you to see your potatoes mature.

There is still another reason why poison sprays and dusts decimate your friends in the garden more quickly than they do your enemies. Pests, over the years, tend to build up an immunity to garden poisons – and even farm poisons.

Pests, like weeds, seem to have a real determination to live and reproduce. But our insect friends in the garden, with their longer reproduction cycles, do not seem to have built up this immunity. They tend to fall victim to the sprays and dusts, which only cuts their number further and reduces their ability to help you with pest control.

We've all heard how the United States has become the breadbasket of the world with the rise of chemical sprays and, indeed, this can be statistically proven. But what would happen if we stopped the massive spraying that gets more extensive and costly each year? With chemical poisons, U. S. agriculture truly has a tiger by the tail.

Widespread crop spraying has become a way of life. We have killed untold numbers of the natural enemies of plant pests: the predators, parasites, bees, birds – and even people! We have produced crops in abundance, and we have government stockpiles to prove it, but at what cost to nature's balance?

Now, whether or not American agriculture is in trouble because of chemical sprays, you would do well to work with nature in your garden. Remember this: We had gardens (and farms – and surpluses) before chemical sprays came into everyday use. And we had many more butterflies then, too. It is true, we had to pick off a few potato bugs; we had to hand-sucker our corn; we had to plant with an eye to controlling pests, and with an understanding of how one plant can help another.

These things may not have been as "efficient" as today's agricultural methods, but, despite this, we still grew our food; we still produced our crops, and you never heard any talk of poisonous water, poisons in the air or pollution.

It's up to you. Garden with or without poisons. The choice is yours. It's your life. It's your health.

Now, whatever method you use, whether it be poisons or working with nature, or a combination of the two, you are still not going to have – nor would you want to have – a simon-pure garden. The garden will have enemies; it will have friends. Keep your purpose in mind: You are not raising a garden to rid the world of plant-eating insects; you are raising a garden for food and for pleasure.

A never-ending war with insects can't be much fun. Keep your purpose in mind. Ask yourself this question: Are the plant-eaters actually destroying, or is the plant continuing to grow and produce? Herbivores are a part of the chain of nature, the building blocks of life for all living things. If these pests are not actually doing harm to you and to your garden, if they are not actually interfering with food production, why poison them?

Your job is not to eliminate. It's to control. Controlling can be done in several ways, the last of which, to our way of thinking, is chemical sprays and dusts.

Gardening is like every other skill; the more you know about it the easier it is. And if you are to garden well, you will actually be controlling the ecosystem in your garden plot. It takes knowledge to do this well.

Start by learning about seeds resistant to the various blights. Read about soil and humus, and how to make compost. Study the ways to mulch, to keep down the work in your garden, and to maintain the proper moisture. Begin at your local library, but don't forget the wealth of information available from your agricultural agent.

Sometimes a garden has a dearth of helping insects, predators and parasites. It's possible to buy ladybugs and praying mantis to bring into your garden for the control of pests. Many people buy them, but if you decide to give it a try, be assured that once the problem has been solved, once the pests are under control, your predators will have to move on in search of food. You can buy them for your garden, but you can't keep them in your garden.

As a purely personal thing, we don't favor this purchase. We prefer to protect those already on the premises. Nature tends to work at maintaining a balance. She will produce predators in relation to prey if given a chance. An imbalance in either direction is something she won't tolerate. Too many plant-eaters and the garden will die, so the pests move on; too many predators and the food supply becomes insufficient, so they, too, move on.

All we should try to do is control – keep a balance.

To be a truly good gardener, you need to develop a new set of reactions. Don't look at a spider or a toad or a mantis with horror. Instead, be pleased to see these valuable links in a natural chain.

It has been a little unfair of us to label these garden denizens as good guys and bad guys. The fact is, they are all good guys; they are all a part of nature's chain. The aphid, for instance, is the food supply for the ladybug. One can't live without the other. All we need to do is keep them in control. It boils down to "keeping a balance."

But suppose you have done companion planting, and you have avoided poison sprays, and you still have a problem of an infestation of one or more insects. You have an imbalance in your garden. What do you do? Your action will depend on which insect is giving the problem. You need to know something about the insect to know how to control it.

Here's where the second pleasure of gardening comes in. You're going to have to read or talk to other gardeners or to your agricultural extension agent. You need to know what kind of conditions the pest needs, how long it lives, how it reproduces, and what natural enemies it has. When you know something about it, you'll know how to proceed.

The ultimate reason for NOT using poisons, either sprays or dust – and this is the most important reason, or at least the most personal – is that you are going to EAT the vegetables you grow. Can you be sure there is no residue of those poisons in or on the fruit? It is a worry to us.

If you must use a poison, try to find out how harmful it is to humankind. The garden supply store may not always be the best place for this information since they make a business of selling poisons, but your agricultural agent should be able to supply you with unbiased information. Ask for it. And, most important of all, READ THE LABELS. Those labels are horror stories, with all sorts of disclaimers and warnings to protect the manufacturer in the event of a lawsuit. Do you still want to use the poisons?

Another method of controlling insect pests is called "trap crops" or "trap planting." With this method you actually plant for the benefit of the pest – you plant something they like better in an area adjacent to the crop you are trying to protect. This is not a method we use, because of space limitations, but it is used extensively by many gardeners – many organic gardeners – because it works.

Mexican beetles, for example, prefer potatoes to beans. So, if you are looking to protect your bean crop, put in an extra row of potatoes in the proximity of your beans, and the beetles will eat the potatoes, and your beans will be left alone. And, who knows, the potatoes may even produce for you, if the plants are healthy enough. Don't plant too close together, however, or the beetles may just decide to nibble on both the beans and the potatoes.

Another example of trap crops might be for flea beetle damage in your garden. If this is the case, plant a row of mustard in the vicinity of your cabbage or eggplant, and the flea beetles will move to the crop they prefer.

Wireworms especially like turnips and radishes, so you might use either of these as your "trap crop." Or, you could use a trap crop of eggplant to lure beetles from your winter supply of potatoes. These are only examples. You will find trap crops for yourself, and still others can be suggested to you by fellow gardeners or county agent.

Using trap crops seems a little like bribing a child to be good, but use the idea if it works for you. Many people are happy with it.

Crop rotation is another good way of cutting down on undesirable insect life. Rotate both your potatoes and tomatoes, because blight is more likely if the same spot is used year after year. Why not rotate all your crops? The enemies of each type of crop tend to be the same year after year. If you plant the same vegetable in the same spot, doesn't it stand to reason that some of the larvae might still be in the soil? It will take more time to plan your garden if you rotate, but what good is January and February, other than studying seed catalogues and planning?

As has been mentioned, toads are great friends in a garden. They will help you control insect population without poisons. Birds will take care of untold numbers of insects. We recommend that you encourage birds by putting a bird bath in or near your garden, and that you keep fresh water in it at all times. Encourage the birds to come for a drink or a bath. It will pay off. Your garden will be healthier and more beautiful.

When it comes to working your garden, the words of Michel de

Montaigne say it concisely and clearly: "Let us permit nature to have her own way; she understands her business better than we do." Work with nature rather than against it. Don't panic at the first sight of an aphid, an earwig or a toad. They are a part of the natural food chain of life. A healthy garden can support a host of good and bad insects and still produce. Healthy plants, like healthy people, can cope with disease or insect attack.

The key is balance. To completely eliminate all harmful insects (and this is not likely), would be to drive off the good insects – those that protect your plants and pollinate them – because their food supply has been removed. You are the control. Your job is to maintain a balance, not to dominate the ecosystem.

You may say, "Interesting, but what has this to do with planting by the sign gardening?"

When you plant by the Moon's signs – when you work with nature, when the moisture for germination is available, when the conditions for sprouting are best – you are in control. And so it is with this chapter. It can be summed up in this way: "As you garden, work with nature, and nature will work with you."

Chart 4 – How To Repel Pests

Pest	Natural Repellent
Ants	Savory
Aphids	Marigolds, Nasturtium, Painted Daisy, Mint, Chives or Garlic (And don't kill ladybugs—they devour aphids.)
Bean Beetle	Rosemary, Sage, Marigolds
Cabbage Worm	Celery, Tomato, Thyme, Sage, Mint, Rosemary, Marigolds (Also, soured milk poured over young cabbage heads is a good deterrent.)
Cabbage Moth	Same as Cabbage Worm (Looks like a yellow butterfly.)
Carrot Flies	Onions, Leeks, Sage, Rosemary
Colorado Potato Beetle	Basil, Green Beans
Cucumber Beetle	Radishes, Savory, Nasturtium, Pansy, Catnip
Flea Beetle	Catnip
Flies or Mosquitoes	Basil
Grasshopper	No specific companion plant, but try to encourage the brown spider in the garden by not poisoning it.
Japanese Beetle	Garlic, Savory, Chives, White Geranium, Zinnia, Castor Beans
Maggots	Onions, Marigolds
Mexican Beetle	Marigolds, Nasturtium, Potatoes
Moles	Castor Beans
Nematodes	Marigolds, or dig Marigold plants, flowers and leaves into the soil.
Other Animal Pests	Tie broken mirror pieces to twirl in the wind, or use Christmas lights or artificial snakes.
Potato Bug	Marigold, Nasturtium
Pumpkin Beetle	Nasturtium

Rabbits	Marigolds, Nasturtium. (Also, bury soft drink bottles, leaving only an inch of the top of the bottle above ground. Even the slightest breeze will create a whistle. You may not hear it, but the rabbit will.)
Raccoons, 'Possums and Squirrels	Plant a barrier crop of soy beans around the garden or the corn field. If this is not possible, plant Nasturtium, Marigolds or Mustard. Another method: dust newly emerging corn silks with cayenne pepper. Repeat if necessary.
Slugs	Lightning bug larvae feed on slugs. Don't discourage lightning bugs with poisons.
Snakes	Gourds on the garden fence
Squash Bugs	Savory, Nasturtium or Marigold
Tomato Worm	Borage or Dill. If they are not otherwise a problem, don't discourage yellow jackets or brachonid wasps.
White Flies	Nasturtium

Chapter 8

Harvesting

Before we get too deeply into this chapter, let's recognize that harvesting can mean anything from a daily picking of your green beans to the taking in of your bounty for winter storage. In this chapter we are thinking more specifically of a harvest that is to be stored for later use. There, the correct Moon phase and sign information is primarily to add to the "keeping" qualities of the harvest.

THE RULE: Harvest in the 3rd or 4th Quarter in Aquarius, Sagittarius or Aries. Any barren sign except Virgo.

First the Moon phase: The gathering of food for later use – harvesting – requires you to pick, dig or reap when the Moon's energies are declining, preferably in the 4th Quarter when the Moon's energies are at their lowest ebb.

The signs of Aquarius, Sagittarius or Aries are preferred because they are the three weakest of the barren signs. This is desirable because the act of harvesting is not meant to destroy the plant, but simply to remove fruit or vegetables with the least possible harm arising from that act. Harvesting sometimes is a continuing process, so the plant should not be harmed by it.

If circumstances or your own time limitations make the use of these three signs impractical, or even impossible, then use Leo or Gemini. In these instances – Aquarius, Sagittarius, Aries, Gemini or Leo – you are harvesting in an air or fire sign, a time when the water content of the bounty is at its lowest. Too much water can cause rot or premature sprouting.

Do you wonder why we recommend harvesting in all barren signs except Virgo? Virgo is an exception in several ways. She is barren; she is the virgin (the non-producer), but she is still a feminine earth sign. So, she is not a dry sign as are the fire and air signs. The moisture in Virgo does not eliminate growth, as the dryness of Leo does. Virgo is barren not because of her moisture, but because of her very nature: The virgin does not produce. So, for harvesting, eliminate the moisture of Virgo which might cause rotting, mildew or sprouting, and opt for the dryness of the barren fire or air signs.

Water content is a very definite factor in storage, so harvesting in the water signs of Cancer, Scorpio or Pisces should never be considered unless you are picking vegetables or fruits for immediate use. These signs should be avoided when you are harvesting for drying, freezing or canning, because the high water content will cause the stored harvest to be less firm.

We realize your garden will have to be picked every day, or every other day at a minimum. We realize, too, that some picking will, of necessity, be done in less than desirable signs and in less than desirable phases of the Moon.

When you are harvesting at less than optimum times, these fruits and vegetables should be cooked, sold or given away, rather than stored.

Let's make this point clear: With garden vegetables that will be dried, frozen or canned, The Rule is less important because of the processing involved. Safe storage is enhanced by processing. When you have something that must be stored for a longer period of time, without processing, The Rule becomes a most important factor.

Potatoes, for example, whether sweet or Irish, are high in water content and are usually stored in open bins without the benefit of processing. Onions, too, would fall into this general category. Your harvest – in the 4th Quarter and in the sign of Aquarius – would stop the potato's growth at a time of minimal water content, so you would have long storage without problems.

If you do not elect to harvest your potatoes in a barren sign and in the waning Moon, expect premature sprouting, well before Spring arrives. Never dig this watery vegetable in the water signs of Cancer, Scorpio or Pisces, except for immediate use.

While the 4th Quarter of the Moon is preferred for the storage of potatoes for table use, because they will keep better and because they will resist sprouting, the 3rd Quarter is preferable if the potatoes are to be used the following Spring as seed potatoes. You want the potatoes to keep, of course, but the 3rd Quarter harvest allows you to dig your potatoes before the Moon has lost all of its power, as would be the case in the 4th Quarter, especially in its last few days. These potatoes will more readily sprout, and will be ready at planting time.

As stated, the digging of your seed potatoes represents a slight variation in The Rule. All the Rules are bendable. You will vary them to obtain specific results. You will alter them depending on the circumstances and the purpose of your harvest, They are meant to be tools, used in various ways, tailored to your needs. Once you are familiar with the reasoning behind each of the Rules, you will be able to work with them, to blend them.

Most of the time when you think of harvesting, you are thinking of food storage, but when storage is not your aim, it might be to your advantage to harvest in the 2nd Quarter. The reason for this is that fruit or vegetables picked during this quarter will be fresher and plumper; they will actually be heavier, and they will have a higher water content. They will not keep as long, but if they are going to the market, then the likelihood is that they will be used within a short period of time, so keeping is not the prime factor.

If you elect to vary The Rule by harvesting in the 2nd Quarter of the Moon, keep in mind that while your bounty will look better, it will be more easily bruised, so care must be taken in the harvest.

Your garden is meant to produce at least three categories of harvest: food for your table, for daily use; food for giving away, or for selling locally; and food for long-term storage. Recognizing the fact that the taking-in of your crops is not a thing that can be postponed, some of your picking is sure to occur in some of the less desirable Moon phases and signs.

When this occurs, as we know it will, try to use those fruits or vegetables for something other than long-term storage, even if processing is involved. The reason for this is that you want to store the best. You want the ripe, firm, perfect fruit in those fruit jars. You will look on them as the work of your own hand; they are, at least to you, works of art. You will, therefore, want to start with the very best raw materials available. This is true of drying or freezing. Firm fruit or vegetables, with a minimum of water content, will process better, and they will have a better appearance when served.

But, whether in the light or dark of the Moon, where possible, harvest in barren signs. This is more important than any other factor. If it is a choice between sign or phase for your harvest, go with a suitable sign. Especially avoid Cancer, Scorpio or Pisces, because they produce water-laden fruits and vegetables that do not keep well and can be easily bruised.

For the harvesting of hay, or any other commodity that requires drying, try to arrange your time so that you can do it during the 4th Quarter of the Moon, in the signs of Aquarius, Aries or Sagittarius. You will find quicker drying, safer storage, and less loss of food value.

If you are drying fruits or vegetables for winter use – and this method of storage is coming back again – use the same principle as with drying hay: Start the drying process during the last quarter of the Moon, after having picked fruits or vegetables in Aquarius, Aries or Sagittarius. Don't pick and wait. You lose food value. Pick and process quickly, whether it be canning, freezing or drying.

Not everyone has an herb garden. But some of us prefer to grow and dry our own aromatics in a separate specific plot, or scattered through our vegetable garden. The harvesting of herbs varies slightly and, therefore, should be mentioned here.

As with all harvesting, Aquarius is best, followed by Sagittarius and Aries. But any barren sign except Virgo will do. It's when you come to Moon phases that a variation exists. Harvest above-ground herbs, parsley, for example, or savory, when the Moon is in the 2nd Quarter. Harvest below-ground herbs when the Moon is in the 3rd or 4th Quarter, which exactly follows The Rule.

There is another interesting thing about the harvesting of herbs. These are things used for seasoning; they are pungent or aromatic, and you want to retain as much of that quality as you can. Gather herbs when the sun is intense, say from 10 or 10:30 in the morning until 3 or 3:30 in the afternoon. This is the time when your herbs – either above or below ground – will be fully energized, so you will be picking or digging them at their prime.

Do any of you hunt for mushrooms anymore? This was widely done in days gone by, but the art of telling the good ones from the bad ones seems to be dying out. When is the best time to go to the pastures or to the woods to gather these delicious "creatures"? Well, apply The Rule where you can, but remember, they are more plentiful and better tasting at the time of the Full Moon. However, if you do hunt for them, be sure you know those that are edible. Many species are poisonous.

As a rule of thumb, we would recommend that all forest harvesting

– whether for lumber, firewood, fence posts or logs – be done in the 3rd or 4th Quarter.

The harvesting of timber or logs is not such an important factor to us individually as it was in days gone by. We now depend on a lumber yard for our needs. But in the old days, when a man cut the logs for his home and farm buildings, when he rived his own shingles, forest harvesting by nature's signs – to prevent rotting or warping – was a real factor.

For the harvesting of firewood, too, you use the last quarter of the Moon, just as you do with hay, and for the same reason – quick drying. It will not only dry more quickly, but you will avoid having worm-eaten firewood. Of course, you must cut the wood in one of the barren signs; Aquarius, Aries or Sagittarius.

Now, another thing about firewood, and it's not always possible to do because of many factors, but if you can, cut firewood for the coming winter in the last quarter of the Moon in January of each year. It will dry with a minimum of shrinkage; it will burn well and it will store without problems.

As long as we are on the subject of firewood, it can be cut in the light of the Moon, and while it may burn brightly, it will not dry properly and, therefore, storage for a longer period of time may not be possible.

Butchering or slaughtering is another kind of "harvesting," but with this job the rules are slightly different. If you butcher in the quarter immediately following the Full Moon (3rd Quarter), the meat will release the fat as it is cooking, basting and tenderizing it as it cooks. The best signs for butchering or slaughtering is Capricorn (the knees) and Pisces (the feet). By using these two signs you get better weight by avoiding shrinkage, and the meat will be firm. AVOID, at all costs, slaughtering when the Moon is in the sign of Leo.

To an extent, another kind of harvesting is the setting of hen eggs. Start the setting when the Moon is in a fruitful sign, preferably in Cancer, but Scorpio and Pisces are also good. Try to time the hatching for a New Moon, or at least a growing Moon. This will produce stronger chicks that will grow more rapidly. From setting to hatching, chicks will take 21 days, ducks 28 and turkeys 30.

As for the date when you start the setting, this can be moved about. The old hen may be anxious, but you can vary the start of the setting until you have a fruitful sign.

The breeding of animals is still another kind of "planting" for harvest. This, too, is a question of timing that is similar to the setting and hatching of eggs. For the animal in question, determine the gestation period. You are looking to have the newborn arrive on or after the New Moon but before the Full Moon. The periods when the animal is ready for breeding (insemination) are not prolonged, so your ability to time the new arrival may be limited, but where possible, for the sake of strong offspring and good, healthy growth (or even for future breeding stock), try to have the newborn's arrival time fall during the light of the Moon (the growing or waxing Moon).

Harvest is the time of gathering, whether this be grains, vegetables or a yield of any type. We have mentioned several. We have tried to make our examples representative. We want you to understand the reasoning behind The Rule, so you will be able to use it in whatever connotation your harvest may be.

We enjoy all facets of the planting or growing process, but it's the harvest that makes the whole thing have meaning.

Chapter 9

Grafting
and
Airlayering

THE RULE: Make the graft during the 1st or 2nd Quarter, in a fruitful sign. Cancer is the first choice, but Scorpio and Pisces are also good.

Grafting, sometimes called budding, is the process of adding a variety, or even varieties, to an already-growing and healthy rootstock. This is done by inserting a shoot of the desired variety into a prepared slit on the host stock – the already-growing and healthy tree or bush. The shoot should be the same size as the host stock, so the tree, when mended, will show no outward sign of the graft.

For example, if you have an apple tree on your property that produces an inferior fruit, or a variety you don't need or especially care for, and if that tree is otherwise healthy, this would be an ideal host for a graft.

We will not try to go into all the details of how this is done. There are a number of books and other sources that are very explicit on the subject in every library, or you can get the information from your county agent, as well as from some of the seed catalogues. We will give you just the rudiments, so that you will understand what the process is, and generally how it is done.

In our example you have an apple tree, a winesap, that produces a fruit that, for whatever reason, you do not like. You would prefer another variety, or even two varieties. Let us suppose you want two yellow apples, a Grimes Golden and a Yellow Delicious. You would select a shoot from each of these two trees, make a slit for each in suitable branches of equal size on the host tree, and you would insert these shoots. Each graft site would then be wrapped and protected until the host tree has assimilated the shoot, giving it renewed life. And, from that point on, all fruit from that branch would be of the variety of the shoot, not the variety of the host tree.

This can be done to any type of apple stock, introducing any kind of shoots. You can buy trees on the market that have five or six varieties already grafted to them by the nursery. These multi-variety trees are mostly for show. Of course, you must stay to type. You would graft apples to apple stock and peaches to peach stock.

There is a real value to grafting. Let us give an example: There is a sour orange that produces an excellent rootstock and tree – strong and disease resistant, easy to cultivate – but the fruit is suitable only for marmalades or orangeade, and only then with the use of lots of sugar or some other type sweetener. On the other hand, there are excellent orange varieties that do not have all the advantages of the sour orange tree because they are not so sturdy, not so resistant. This is a perfect "marriage"; grafting is the answer.

Now let's go back and examine The Rule. It is easy to understand the reason for using a fruitful sign, since you are grafting to produce something, to make new life. But why choose the 1st and 2nd Quarters of the Moon?

For a moment, consider the other two choices, the 3rd and 4th Quarters of the Moon. Start with the least desirable. The 4th Quarter is the last seven days of a dying Moon, the lowest energy level. This is a fine time for destroying any unwanted growth; and it would, therefore, seem hardly the prime time for creating growth.

What about the 3rd Quarter? It is good for root crops, but you are grafting new life here, not producing roots. As a matter of fact, you are utilizing roots that were grown at some other time – fully matured roots – so the strength of the 3rd Quarter of the Moon is a strength you don't need with grafting.

The 3rd and 4th Quarters of the Moon are periods of decreasing energy, just as the size of the Moon that you see is decreasing; it is a time of shrinkage. Because of this, even if the graft is done in a fruitful sign, you will run the risk of ruining your graft because the host tree may have failed to accept it.

So, by process of elimination, you have the 1st and 2nd Quarters. But there are more reasons than just the fact that you have eliminated the other two quarters. In the first two quarters, the Moon is growing in strength; it is vital. That power is useful in healing the wound you made when you cut off a branch, made a slit, and inserted the new shoot. In the 1st or 2nd Quarter you have a time when the host tree will expand around it and nurture the shoot.

All grafting should be done in the 1st or 2nd Quarter of the Moon, but it is desirable to do it as early as possible after the New Moon. This is a time of high energy, or growing energy, but you have an added plus when you get the job done early in the period: You are allowing a longer period for the shoot to become established before the Moon begins to decline in strength.

In The Rule we recommend a fruitful sign, but a semi-fruitful sign will do, and there are people who actually prefer to use Capricorn. Why is this? Their explanation boils down to the tenacity that Capricorn brings. They feel that this sign will hold the bud, will fuse it firmly into the host tree. We have no argument with that.

One more thing about grafting. It is best done in the Spring. This period of time will vary from one part of the country to another, but, generally, it is March through May. When the tree is dormant, when the sap is down, you can prevent excessive bleeding. This, too, is an excellent time for any pruning or shaping required. It prevents shock to the tree. Very early Spring is excellent.

Airlayering is a method of producing many plants from a single host. You do not change variety; you produce more plants of the same variety. Many plants or shrubs will grow from a slip planted in the ground if it is kept watered, or will even put out roots in a can of water, but it is not always the most desirable way of getting additional plants, and it certainly is not the fastest way to get larger plants. Airlayering is the answer.

So, how is it done?

With airlayering, you are attempting to grow a new shrub from an existing one, making a larger and more mature plant than you could get from a cutting. Select a branch with foliage of the desired size. Look for a spot on the existing shrub that will not be noticeable when the airlayered plant is removed. Take care in choosing the branch.

Using a very sharp knife, make two cuts completely around the branch – girdle it – approximately an inch to an inch-and-a-half apart. The distance apart will depend on the size of the branch – the larger the branch the wider the cut. Be sure that you cut through both layers of bark, right down to the hard wood.

Now, scrape away all vestiges of both the outer and inner bark. This is most important. If any part of either layer remains, the shrub will continue to supply life to the selected limb, which will make your attempt useless. All energy to the limbs goes through these two layers of bark, so be sure they are removed. Once you have scraped away *both* layers, the branch will be dependent on the moisture you are supplying.

With your cut made, with all traces of the two layers of bark removed, wrap a wad of water-soaked sphagnum moss around the wound. Wrap clear plastic around this ball of moss, thus forming an airtight covering around the wound and the moss. This plastic wrapping is then tied securely at the top and bottom with wire or plastic twisters. You now have a plastic container holding all of the wet moss against the wound. This branch – soon to be your new plant – will draw all its moisture, its life, from the wet moss, and it will grow roots at this spot.

It will take about three weeks or more (depending on the type host plant) for a complete set of new roots to form at this moss-wrapped wound site. As these roots grow, they will push through the moss so that you can see them through the plastic. After you have a good root system, cut the limb off below the wound site, and transplant it to a permanent location. From that point on it will require only adequate watering to give it a good start.

You will have a live and growing plant of the desired height and it will not, as a general rule, lose any of its leaves during this process. If you have bought shrubs recently, you know how expensive they are. With airlayering, you can use one host for many new plants, providing you are judicious in the removal of these plants.

Some gardeners feel that a newly-rooted plant is not strong enough to supply sufficient nourishment for its own survival. Because of this, when the new plant is ready, they prune at least a third of it on the theory that there is less work for the root system to do until the plant is reestablished in its new environment. (This is always recommended by fruit and nut tree suppliers, and sometimes they pre-prune for the buyer.) Based on our experience, the trimming process is not essential when reproduction is by airlayering.

Most texts on airlayering will instruct you to saw or clip the branch from the host plant just below the "rootball," the moss mass. This works fine. It was the way we started our experiments with airlayering, but at the time we were learning the technique we were living in South Florida where many of the plants have abundant and large leaves. And, unless you trim back severely, the wind will move the new plant, damaging the fragile new roots.

We started cutting the new plant six or eight inches below the rootball, burying this entire thing in the ground, so that the extra six to eight inches would act as an additional anchor, a stabilizer, and we had better results because the wind could not ruin new plants before they grew sturdy on their own.

The extra six to eight inches of branch below the rootball will not add to the growth of the plant in any way. It is used only as a stabilizer, a support for the upper leafy part of the plant, to protect delicate roots until they have taken hold in their new environment.

With this method in mind, when do you begin the airlayering and when do you cut it off the host plant or shrub for transplanting? Here again, you should begin the job in a fruitful sign, in the light of the Moon (1st or 2nd Quarter). You are looking for a strong root system on the new shrub, so we recommend Pisces as a first choice, with Cancer second and Scorpio third. In the instance of airlayering, the water signs are much more desirable than the two fruitful earth signs of Taurus and Capricorn.

When the time comes to remove the new shrub from its host and to transplant it, follow the rule of all good transplanting: Choose a fruitful sign and a growing Moon where possible.

We know a nurseryman in South Florida, an expert in airlayering. He uses the 1st and 2nd Quarters, but he also uses the seven days following the Full Moon. We wondered about this, since most authorities prefer the 1st or 2nd Quarter. He explained it this way: "I'm in the business of raising and selling plants. There are times when I can't afford the luxury of waiting for optimum conditions. I try to do all my airlayering in the fruitful signs, because I have better results. But, because I can't always get all the work done within that fourteen-day period, I reasoned that since the 3rd Quarter was best for root crops, and since I was interested in roots with my airlayering, why not give it a try. I have had good results, so now I use all three: 1st, 2nd and 3rd. But I never use the last quarter of the Moon; the results just aren't there."

The method we have described is not the only method of airlayering, of course, nor is it necessarily the best, but it is the one we have used successfully. Before trying it for the first time, please go to your library or see your county agent. Both are excellent sources.

In addition to airlayering, there is "layering," a slightly different method of getting new plants from host plants. This works well with grapes, roses, and berries of various types, and we feel sure many other plants we have not experimented with to date. Here again, we have given only the rudiments, so that you can grasp the idea. We recommend that you do further reading before giving it a try. Our aim here is not to tell you how this is done, but to tell you when to do it for best results, by both the sign and the phase of the Moon.

Briefly, when you layer, you pull one of the lower branches or canes down to the ground and secure it with a mound of earth. The branch or cane should not be broken. The tip of the cane or branch is left out of the ground. Let it form new roots. This will take some time. It is best to do this in late summer or fall, and in the Spring you will have newly-rooted plants. Remove the newly formed plant.

Let's recap it: Use the first two phases of the Moon (or even the 3rd) for all airlayering, layering, and even the rooting of slips, being sure that you use one of the fruitful or semi-fruitful signs: Cancer, Scorpio, Pisces, Taurus or Capricorn. Capricorn, while only semi-fruitful and at almost the bottom of the pecking order, has the saving advantage of being ruled by Saturn. With the Saturn you can expect honest reward for honest effort. If you are going to go at the job half-heartedly, then avoid doing this while the Moon is in the sign of Capricorn, and stay with the three most fruitful signs mentioned above.

Chapter 10

Elsewhere Around
The Home

One single rule covering all subjects in this chapter is not possible. Each subheading has a rule that applies to one particular section of the chapter. The subheadings, listed alphabetically, are: Baking, Canning-Freezing-Drying, Castration, Dehorning, Reproduction, Slaughtering and Weaning.

As you look to a specific section, look there, too, for The Rule that applies to it.

Planting is one of the major focuses of this book, but planting is more than just putting a seed in the ground. It is a word that has many shades of meaning, and we will look at those other analogous areas. Planting, for example, is surely a first cousin to "implanting," or "reproduction," one of the subheadings we will be considering.

In this chapter we will deal with using the phases of the Moon and the signs for a variety of activities around the house, the barn, the outbuildings, the fields and the gardens.

To paraphrase, "Man does not live by tomato alone," so we will use the Moon phases and the signs in all other aspects of the homestead. These activities, we think, are part of the "gardening concept." In one way or another, they contribute to production, even if the primary action is actual destruction. Cutting a lawn, for example, is primarily an act of destruction, but it contributes mightily to the growth and appearance of that lawn. Castration, certainly, is an act of destruction, but it is an important part of beef production.

In its own way, each subject contributes to production, if only indirectly, and, therefore, can and should be considered. With that said, we will look at the subheadings one by one, in alphabetical order.

Baking

THE RULE: Where possible, bake on a growing Moon phase (1st or 2nd Quarter), in a fruitful sign, especially if the baked goods need to rise.

We are well aware of the fact that today's modern yeasts, baking powders and sodas are vastly superior to those that grandma had to cope with, but all the same, when you take the time to bake something in the oven, you want it to be the best you can possibly make.

So, let's examine The Rule. In baking, the Moon phase is actually less important than the Moon sign, with the possible exception of a souffle or bread, or even puff pastries, where considerable expansion is desired. Here, the action of a growing Moon is beneficial.

As for the Moon signs, it depends on what you wish to achieve. Libra would be a good sign for fancy cookies or for any baked goods destined for display at the fair. Libra lends something special to any items of beauty, whether it's flowers in your garden or food on your table.

But many of the fruitful or semi-fruitful signs are good for baking: Cancer, Scorpio, Pisces, Taurus or Capricorn. And there is one more: Aries. Because of the "action" of its ruling planet Mars, Aries will impart that energy to the baked goods. Even though it is not fruitful, Aries may be used successfully. This means that you actually have a choice of seven two-and-a-half-day periods to choose from – more than enough choices to give you a suitable baking day for any week in the year.

Of the seven signs listed above, four are especially good because they are called "movable" signs. They each have a special "action" quality which will improve the action of your leavening agent, whatever it may be. These four signs are the Cardinal signs: Aries, Cancer, Libra and Capricorn. As noted, Aries is not a fruitful sign, but it is an "action" sign, and it is a movable sign.

You have plenty of latitude, plenty of available days when you will have a functional sign for baking.

As a quick review, here are the good baking signs: Cancer, Scorpio, Pisces, Taurus, Capricorn, Libra and Aries. And, since each sign covers a period of roughly two-and-a-half days, you will have seventeen-and-a-half days out of each twenty-eight-day Moon cycle that are favorable for baking. Bon Appétit!

Canning, Freezing, Drying

THE RULE: For canning, use the waning Moon where possible (3rd or 4th Quarter) in a fruitful sign; for drying, begin as early as possible in the waning Moon, barren fire sign: Leo, Aries, or Sagittarius.

So much for The Rule. Let's look at this subject in detail, so we can understand why The Rule exists.

More people can fruits and vegetables from their gardens than any other method of preserving. So, let's start with that phase of garden storage.

Without exception, all preserving of the garden's bounty – whether by canning, drying or freezing – is best done when the Moon has passed Full and is in its fourteen-and-a-half-day period of "declining energy" – the dark of the Moon. When you are ready to store your food, there is no longer a need for growth. All of your produce or fruit should have been picked at its peak condition, and you will be putting those foodstuffs to rest, so to speak, until the day arrives when they will be used at your table. Your fruits and vegetables, regardless of the method used, are now going "on hold," and that's the reason the waning Moon is best.

Productive gardens, however, do not always permit perfect timing. There will be occasions when you must store the fruits of your labors. You can't let them become overripe. You are always going to choose fruits or vegetables that are fully ripe and unblemished. If you have a harvest that meets these specifications, that must be taken care of during a growing Moon phase, get on with the job. The actual growth is over and the phase is not as important as the sign. So much for the Moon phase.

In choosing the sign for canning or freezing, you have a wide latitude. Use the fruitful signs of Cancer, Scorpio or Pisces; use the semifruitful signs of Taurus or Capricorn, or use the sign of Libra – particularly Libra if beauty is an important factor.

As usual, we like to explain why these signs are used. It's always easier to follow a procedure if you are aware of the reasons behind it. The fruitful signs listed above are water signs. They will keep your produce from losing the natural moisture in the canning or freezing process.

Taurus, the first of the semi-fruitful signs, is a natural for storage, because it is by nature a collector of assets. As an example, among other things, Taurus rules banking, money, possessions, treasuries – even wallets. You see how this fits. When you process food you are storing your assets. Your canned goods – especially with today's prices – are a valued asset. And Taurus also rules storerooms. You see how this ties in. From your storehouse will come those great things to eat in the winter months.

The second of the semi-fruitful signs is Capricorn. This is a sign that by its very nature denotes permanence. There is, also, with Capricorn, a very definite tie-in with farms, fields and gardens. It is the ruler of the preservation of food. Capricorn is concerned with the sustaining of life. We are, once again, back to the word "permanence." Capricorn speaks of rewards for work well done. And isn't this canning?

Libra would be the choice for canned goods destined for the fair. With Libra you can make harmonious arrangements within the jar; you can bring out the beauty of your canning before anyone ever tastes its goodness.

We have spoken here of the canning of fruits and vegetables. These are the most common things found in glass jars, but, at butchering time meat can also be canned. Freezing has almost stopped the canning of meat. But, years ago, this method of preserving meats was widely used.

One good thing about having your meats canned: if the power goes off from a wintertime ice storm, you won't worry about losing it.

It's true that the canning of meat has become almost a lost art, but why not try it – on a limited basis – just to see how it works, and also because your freezer capacity has a limit.

When you are putting up jellies, jams and preserves, you don't want a "watery" result. The best possible signs for this task are not the water signs of Cancer or Pisces, as so often have been recommended for other types of storage. Instead use the fixed signs of Scorpio, Taurus, or even Aquarius. These will help hold the proper consistency, so that your jelly won't be runny or the jams won't weep. It's true that Scorpio is a water sign, but it is acceptable here because it's a fixed sign; it will give form to the product. Aquarius is recommended for the same reason.

For the pickling process, the 3rd or 4th Quarter of the Moon is best, just as with all other canning or freezing. And, here again, as with jelly and jam, the fixed signs are preferable. Taurus, Scorpio or even Aquarius will give you firm, crisp pickles, while water signs will give a less desirable result.

As we did research for this book, we talked to a great many people about their experiences, and about the lore that had been handed down to them. In several instances we reported those experiences or those bits of inherited lore without recommending them. Here is an example:

We found a number of people who expressed a preference for pickling in the sign of Aries. We can see no logical reason for this choice. It is a barren Cardinal fire sign and offers nothing to the preserving process of the pickles, to their crispness, to the water content, or their flavor. Use this sign for pickling if you like, or experiment with it, but we do not recommend it.

Drying fruits and vegetables is an old art. For a time – at least for the home gardener – it all but died out. It was too much trouble, especially when freezing came along, or after pressure cookers made canning easier and safer. But now, thank goodness, drying seems to be making a comeback. The reason for the resurgence may be the newer methods of drying, with electric ovens for this specific purpose. Or, possibly home drying is coming back because "you are in control here," you control the additives; you know the quality of the food you are storing for your family.

Drying, in the old days, was a chore. We can remember it: The clean, white bedsheet on the tin roof of the barn lean-to, where all the peeled and sliced apples were spread out in the sun and wind as the drying process proceeded. This was not done quickly, as it can be done now in the modern food drying ovens. In those days, it was a several-day process, with the slices being turned so that all sides would be exposed to the sun and air. The fruit had to be brought in at night and then taken back out and rearranged the next day. And you had to keep a sharp eye for a sudden summer shower, giving yourself enough time to bring in the fruit before it got wet.

With today's methods, the guesswork has been taken out. Controlled temperature makes the process continuous.

Today drying results are uniform and excellent. In earlier days the weather was a real factor. Because of dew at nightfall or dawn, because of rain, the process was sporadic. The proper dryness of your finished product became more of an art than a science; it was something you learned from experience. If, for example, you failed to sufficiently dry your produce, it would mildew as it hung in the storage bag. All that hard work had to be destroyed because it was not fit for human consumption.

Keep in mind the one big plus factor you have here: In your canning, freezing or drying, *you* are in control, so you know the quality of the vegetable or fruit; you know the cleanliness of the storing process; you know that you have added no harmful preservatives or additives. None of these "questionable things" with "funny names" have been added to your food supply.

Now, let's talk about how and when. If possible, drying should be done on a waning Moon, as it decreases in size and loses its energy. As with canning and freezing, the phase of the Moon is not of paramount importance, but utilize it when you can. For drying, the best choices are the fire signs: Leo, Aries and Sagittarius. The air signs: Gemini, Aquarius and Libra are good second choices.

If you elect to do old-fashioned drying, relying on the sun and the wind, be sure to start the process as soon after the Full Moon as possible, so you will have plenty of time. With the newer ovens specifically for drying, this is not a critical point.

Before we leave this subject, however, we must mention that successful drying can be done in the oven of your kitchen stove. It requires very low heat. With a gas stove, the pilot light is often enough. This will require some experimentation. Cost is a factor, but if it were not, special drying ovens are preferable.

Thus far, nothing has been said about freezing. As concerns using the phases of the Moon or its signs for this process, we found little of value as we did our research. We have had to approach the subject of freezing using only our own logic. In our minds, neither the phase of the Moon nor its sign would make much difference when you are freezing food for storage. After all, there is no processing that might cause flavor loss, except, of course, for blanching. Freezing is a method that puts the fruit or vegetable on hold. Within limits, it will keep perfectly until you are ready to use it.

As is the case with the harvesting of all foods for storage, pick only perfect, fully-matured vegetables or fruits for the freezing process. Anything that does not meet these criteria should become tablefare. How long will it keep? Well, each food has its own set of limitations, so you would be wise to get this information from your local farm extension office or home demonstration agent, or look in your freezer book. It contains a wealth of information. The key here could be the water content of the fruit or vegetable to be frozen.

Strawberries, for example, are high in water content, and, while they may be frozen, they tend to deteriorate in appearance when thawed. With any of the watery fruits or vegetables, you are going to have to have a deterioration.

In such cases, wouldn't it be wise to avoid the water signs for freezing? We would use the fixed signs for freezing, because they will tend to preserve the firmness of the food, just as they do with jellies and jams. We did not find this in our research, but it does seem logical. So, if the water content is high, avoid Cancer and Pisces when possible, and use the fixed signs of Taurus, Scorpio or Aquarius. Where water content is not a problem, such as with peas or beans, any of the fruitful signs may be used.

Here's another thing to keep in mind with watery fruits or vegetables. If you pick them after a rain, especially in a water sign, you will find that their water content is increased considerably. Accordingly, deterioration of appearance will be even more accented. This additional water will also decrease, or "water down," the flavor.

As you grow more familiar with the pluses and minuses of the Moon's phases and signs, perhaps you'll want to experiment with the fruits and vegetables you freeze. Mark the packages carefully so you'll know the phase and sign at the time of picking and freezing. Then check the quality, condition and flavor of the produce as you use it.

Castration

THE RULE: Use the 4th Quarter or the 1st Quarter phase of the Moon for minimizing bleeding, and perform this procedure in Capricorn, Aquarius, Pisces, Aries, Taurus, Gemini or Cancer.

This is The Rule most often cited for castration, neutering, or any type of surgery. There is good reason for it, but it is not the only theory that has logic behind it. We will, however, examine the entire subject. Every facet will be considered.

First, the Moon's phases and then the signs.

One school of thought favors the 4th and 1st Quarters of the Moon because that is the 14- to 15-day period in the Moon's 28-day-plus cycle when it is at the farthest possible point from the Full Moon (the period when bleeding is at its greatest). The theory is that you avoid the Full Moon because of its effect on all fluids of the earth, human or animal blood included. The Full Moon tends to expansion and, therefore, excess bleeding. From that point of view, just before or after the New

Moon would be the ideal time for surgery, with a minimum of blood loss.

Another theory concerning the Moon's phases for the purpose of castration – or any other type of surgery – is that it should be done on a growing Moon, 1st and 2nd Quarters, taking care to stay as much before the Full Moon as possible. The 1st Quarter, therefore, would be preferable. Now, why the growing Moon? The theory here is that it's a time of growing energy, which would speed the healing process. Using this theory, stay as far away as possible from the Full Moon, because of the bleeding.

Those who prefer the 4th and 1st Quarters will often cite a study by Dr. Edson J. Andres, who analyzed the records of one thousand tonsillectomies. He found that only 18 percent experienced hemorrhaging when the surgery was done in the 4th or 1st Quarters of the Moon – well away from the Full Moon. Dr. Andres' study is not the only one concerning excessive bleeding at the time of a Full Moon.

Use either Moon phase theory. Both, however, make one single point crystal clear: Avoid elective surgery near the Full Moon.

Now, Moon signs. Keep this in mind: Any surgical procedure is best performed when the sign the Moon is in has moved well beyond the sign of the affected area – in other words, well beyond the sign that governs the site of the surgery. Therefore, with castration or neutering, you are talking about surgery to the sex organs (Scorpio). This would eliminate Scorpio and Libra (kidney and ovaries). And then, for good measure, we would eliminate the sign before Libra, which is Virgo, and the sign after Scorpio, which is Sagittarius (bowels and liver).

As stated, the signs to be avoided for surgical castration are: Virgo, Libra, Scorpio and Sagittarius. To this list, add one more: Leo, ruling the heart. As a matter of fact, eliminate Leo for all surgical procedures, except in an emergency, when there is no choice.

In the past, castration was surgically done. In recent years this job is being done more and more by what is commonly called the "rubber band" method, where the blood flow to the testes is cut off by a tight rubber band, or similar device, that blocks the blood supply from the body to the testes, causing atrophy. In this case, as with castration, your bull becomes a steer.

We mention this because surgery is not involved, and there is no risk of excessive bleeding. With this method, the Moon phase becomes less important, although the 3rd or 4th Quarter would be excellent, for it is a time of declining energy, and would hasten the process.

The sign the Moon is in, however, is still a factor, and we would continue to avoid those signs more closely related to the site of the procedure, i.e., Virgo, Libra, Scorpio and Sagittarius. And, as is logical in such a case, the barren signs of Aquarius, Aries or Gemini could also be factors in hastening the process.

Before we leave this subject, there is one other question that arises. If the rubber band procedure or actual surgery is to be performed to the sex organs, why eliminate one sign before Libra (kidneys or ovaries) and one sign after Scorpio (sex organs)? A great deal of this information was taken from almanacs – some of them quite old – and since there was no easy formula given for ascertaining the arrival of a sign in any given area of the country, by forbidding the use of the sign before and the sign following the affected area (the surgery site), you lessen the chances of an error in sign, and thus a failure or other complication.

In the back of this book, under GLOSSARY, we have given an easy way to correct your almanac's time to your own local time. With a little computation, you could safely use both Libra and Sagittarius.

Dehorning Animals

THE RULE: Use the 4th or 1st Quarter of the Moon, in any sign other than Pisces, Aries or Taurus.

Here again, as with the previous section on Castration, you may use the 4th and 1st Quarters to prevent bleeding, or use the 1st and 2nd Quarters, so long as you avoid the Full Moon or the several days that precede the Full Moon.

And, as with the section on castration, the 4th and 1st Quarters prevent excessive bleeding, and the 1st and 2nd Quarters promote healing.

If you are dehorning and have not read the section of this chapter on Castration, please do. A more complete explanation of the Moon's phases is made there.

When dehorning, note that in The Rule you have one sign before the affected area, which is Aries – the head – and one sign after it that are not recommended. For that reason, Aries, the site of the procedure, is eliminated, along with Pisces and Taurus, the sign preceding and following. (See Castration for a full explanation of this recommendation.)

Again, when dehorning, any of the Moon signs, other than Pisces, Aries and Taurus, may be used, but we recommend the avoidance of

Leo (the heart) on general principles, and we would further recommend the use of the barren signs (Gemini, Virgo, Sagittarius, Aquarius) rather than the fruitful signs (Cancer, Libra, Scorpio and Capricorn). A barren sign is less likely to produce regrowth.

Castration (unless the rubber band method is used) and Dehorning are only two of the many surgical procedures that may be required on domestic animals. The principle is the same for all of them. We would recommend that you read the section on Surgery in Chapter 14, Miscellany.

Reproduction

THE RULE: Time breeding to produce births in the 1st or 2nd Quarter of the Moon, and in a fruitful or semi-fruitful sign.

This Rule needs to be enlarged upon because the purpose of breeding is not always the same. For example, are you breeding to acquire future breeding stock, animals for the market, or are you looking to breed for show? In each instance you might choose a different timing so that the birth would occur in a sign suitable for the particular purpose.

Fortunately, the gestation period for domestic animals is not as variable as it is for human beings. When you set hen eggs, for example, you can expect the hatching of the chicks to occur in 21 days. When you breed a sow, you can expect piglets in 113-114 days. This, of course, makes timing a factor that you can deal with.

Much of the breeding of farm animals is now being done by artificial insemination. There are a variety of reasons for this – a champion bull, located three states away, can be the sire of your intended breeding stock. The point is that timing is made even more plausible by the rise of artificial insemination techniques.

Even so, timing can be "iffy." Some animals are ready for breeding for only a short period of time. A cow, for example, has a fertile period of only 24 to 72 hours, and will accept the bull for only about half of that period. The control you have over your breeding stock is far from perfect, but it is still worth making the effort.

All we are suggesting is that you work with nature to produce the finest and most desirable results. When you use the Moon phases and signs you are working with nature, but, as every farmer knows, nature does not always work with you.

The first factor mentioned in The Rule is the phase of the Moon. For the health, strength and growth of your new animals, try to breed so that they are born in the 1st or 2nd Quarter of the Moon. You have a fairly good chance of receiving nature's cooperation with this factor, because one-half of the 28-day-plus cycle of the Moon is available. You have a 50-50 chance. This roughly 14-day period of the 1st and 2nd Quarters of the Moon is when the Moon is growing in strength and light. It will impart those qualities to the newborn.

Random breeding should give you a success rate of 50 percent. With a little pre-planning, and with proper timing insofar as it is possible, you should be able to bring this success rate up to 80 or 90 percent, thus giving your newborns the advantage of a 1st or 2nd Quarter birth.

The timing of a birth for a specific sign, a specific two-and-a-half-day period, requires a good deal more from you, but it's far from impossible. We acknowledge that luck is a larger factor here. It's worth an effort.

For the purpose of illustration, we will use cattle, but the same principles apply to other animals or fowl. Births that occur when the Moon is in the fruitful signs of Cancer, Scorpio or Pisces will give you good breeding stock. They will, in other words, be "fruitful" animals, although perhaps not always the sturdiest.

If the breeding is being done for meat production, when it's possible, time the birth for the earth signs of Taurus or Capricorn. These are the signs that stress the practical and sustaining side of the breeding process. These two signs will produce lean animals that will more quickly grow to maturity. These will be sturdier animals.

As we have said before in other applications, if you are breeding for show, for gracefulness, for well-proportioned animals, try to time the birth for the sign of Libra.

Slaughtering

THE RULE: This kind of "harvest" is best done after the Full Moon. The 3rd Quarter is best, but the 4th is acceptable. Capricorn (the knees) or Pisces (the feet) are the best signs.

Let's first consider the Moon's phases. If you use the 3rd and 4th Quarters – when the Moon is decreasing and losing its strength – your meat, when cooked, will release its stored fat more readily, and this release of fat will give you a more tender meat.

As stated in The Rule, the signs of Capricorn and Pisces are ideal for slaughter. You will get firm meat, with a minimum of shrinkage as it is cooked. Your schedule, for whatever reason, may not allow you to use these two signs. If that is the case, then we suggest the following, in descending order: Aquarius, Aries, Taurus, Sagittarius, Gemini, Scorpio. Be aware, however, that our first recommendation is Capricorn or Pisces. Strive for these two signs in a waning phase of the Moon. At all costs, avoid Leo for slaughtering. Any choice would be better than this barren, fixed, fire sign.

Weaning

THE RULE: Wean on a waning Moon, 3rd or 4th Quarter, in the sign of Sagittarius, Capricorn, Aquarius or Pisces.

First, the Moon's phase. The recommended time is when the Moon is losing its strength. Actually, the 4th Quarter is better than the 3rd because these energies are at their lowest ebb during that phase of the 28-day Moon cycle. As you no doubt recall, the Moon rules fluids. Milk is a fluid. Not only is it less available during the dark of the Moon, but the offspring's need will be less at this time, so another source of food can be offered.

With weaning, you are breaking a habit. This is not just a run-of-the-mill habit. It's a life-giving habit, so you are going to have to be careful in choosing the Moon's sign. The weaning process will not be easy, so work with nature by selecting both a good phase and sign.

You may have noted that the Moon signs given in The Rule seem to have been chosen at random – they are not all fruitful, nor are they all barren. At first glance they seem to have no pattern at all, but this, of course, is not the case. Sagittarius, Capricorn, Aquarius and Pisces are several signs away from those parts of the animal (or person) most affected by the weaning process, most affected by the change in eating habits – and, indeed, the eating content – that is being forced upon the young animal.

What you are doing here is avoiding those signs that could make the job more difficult. You are avoiding the signs of Gemini (the nervous system), Cancer (the stomach), Leo (the heart) and Virgo (the bowels). You can readily see how these things fit into the feeding cycle, and how avoiding a disturbance here could make the weaning process easier for the animal and you.

We listed the preferred weaning signs as Sagittarius, Capricorn, Aquarius and Pisces, and this is in descending order. There is good reason for this, too. As with castration or dehorning, you want the first suitable and available sign after the Moon has left the sign that governs the affected part.

With the weaning process we are avoiding four consecutive signs: Gemini, the nervous system; Cancer, the stomach; Leo, the heart; and Virgo, the bowels. The first available and still suitable sign after these four is Sagittarius. It is the most desirable because it will take more signs of approximately two-and-a-half days each before the Moon enters the first sign to be avoided in weaning, which is, of course, Gemini, the nervous system. At best, weaning is a difficult process for the calf. Avoiding upsetting the nervous system of the animal is certainly desirable.

Five signs of approximately two-and-a-half days each will give you about twelve-and-a-half days that the animal will be on the new feeding regime. That is a substantial period in a young animal's life. The length of the period will depend on when, in Sagittarius, the weaning was actually begun. The calf will be getting used to the new feeding procedures; it will be more adjusted before the Moon gets back to the sign that could cause upset to the nervous system.

With Capricorn you still have a reasonably long period of time, four signs of two-and-a-half days each, before the Moon is back entering the sign of Gemini, the nervous system. And, if the weaning process must be delayed until Aquarius, you lose another two-and-a-half-day period. When you get to the sign of Pisces to begin the weaning, you only have a period of about five days before the animal's nervous system is highlighted by the Moon's entrance into Gemini.

You can see the advantage of starting the weaning as early as possible in that series of consecutive signs: Sagittarius, Capricorn, Aquarius or Pisces.

There is still another good reason why Sagittarius is the best choice for weaning. Ideally, the last feeding by the mother should be in a fruitful sign. Sagittarius is preceded by a fruitful sign, making this ideal condition a real possibility. It also has the added advantage of being farthest removed from those four signs that could make weaning more difficult for the animal: Gemini, Cancer, Leo and Virgo.

It is true that Aquarius is also preceded by a semi-fruitful sign (Capricorn), but it does not allow as many days to pass before arriving at the first sign (Gemini) that could complicate the weaning process. Weaning, as with all the other things in this book, is made easier by working with nature, working with the natural cycle of the Moon's twenty-eight-day journey through the signs.

This, too, might be considered a weaning process. If you are think-ing of going on a diet, Sagittarius is a good choice for the first day, and for much the same reasons: You are altering your intake of food. You could be upsetting your nervous system; your stomach; perhaps not your heart, but at least your heart's desire; and, your bowels. We may not like to think of ourselves as animals, but we are, and a change in dietary habits is not easy to cope with. While this is not as difficult for us as it is for a young animal, it is, nevertheless, a thing that could be upsetting to our nervous system.

In the back of this book, in the Glossary, there is a drawing of the human body, showing the parts that correspond with each of the Moon's signs. In addition, for the sake of clarity, we have another chart – a pie-shaped wheel – numbered 1 through 12. As you start with No. 1, the head, and proceed through the numbers, you will see the exact order that the Moon follows as it proceeds through the signs in each 28-day-plus cycle. By looking at this wheel or the drawing of the hu-man body, you will better understand why Sagittarius is farthest re-moved from Gemini, which is as it should be for the weaning process.

You may have noticed that we did not mention Libra and Scorpio on one side of the wheel, and Aries and Taurus on the other side. We simply used the four signs exactly opposite from the four detrimental signs. We were looking for distance, for signs as far removed from the detrimental signs as possible. If you will look at the wheel you can see why this was done.

With Weaning, we complete Elsewhere Around The Homestead. Insofar as possible, we have dealt with those things that directly or in-directly contribute toward a harvest, or a laying-by of the bounty. There are other subjects in Chapter 14, Miscellany, which are pertinent, although they apply less directly to either planting or harvesting. Please refer to the Miscellany chapter for such ancillary things as Buying a Farm, House, Livestock or Farm Machinery. There is also a subsection on Painting, Lawn Care, Surgery, Vision, Hair Care, and many other things not connected to the homestead, per se.

Chapter 11

Why It Works: Cycles

CYCLES: There are natural laws that govern all life on earth, and possibly life in the universe as well. These natural laws are easiest viewed as cycles. So, what is a cycle? It has been defined as: "An orderly process of change which returns to the point at which it began."

The most common cycle is the earth's rotation on its axis. This gives us a very familiar cycle: dawn, midday, dusk and midnight, and then a new dawn – a complete cycle. Or, consider the cycle of the earth as it revolves around the Sun. This gives you the cycle of the seasons: Spring, Summer, Autumn and Winter.

A third common cycle, the one we are concerned with here, is the Moon's 28-day-plus journey around the earth. On that journey it passes through each of the twelve signs. The impact of that cycle can be seen on the fluids of the earth. One well-known result is the oceans' tides. Another might be a seed's absorption of water.

As the earth revolves on its axis, we have a period of light and a period of darkness – a day and a night. The Moon revolving around the earth produces a similar cycle. The two weeks from New Moon to Full Moon (the so-called light of the Moon, or waxing) could be compared with our day, and the two weeks following the Full Moon (the dark of the Moon, or waning), could be likened to our night.

The active, energetic "daylight" periods, when the Moon is growing, is when most planting is done, especially those things that will produce a crop above the ground.

Plant root-bearing crops during the "night" phases of the Moon because a regenerative process is taking place in the earth, below sight, in the root system. This is also the time to plant bulbs or perennials, or biennials – anything that depends on its root system to sustain it during the period of little or no growth – the fall and winter, for example. Here the "hidden" aspect is again accented, the "below the earth" aspect – the dark side of the plant, its roots. In each of these things – bulbs, tubers, perennials – it is the strength of that hidden aspect of the plant that is vital; it is the strength of the roots.

While we are on the subject of this 28-day-plus cycle of the Moon, keep in mind that it is divided into more than just the "day" and "night" phases or the four quarters. It is also divided into twelve periods, each approximately two-and-a-half days long, as the Moon moves through the signs.

In gardening, and in all other aspects of life, each of these twelve, by the very nature of the sign, offers advantages and disadvantages. You will seek to utilize these factors. You will combine the nature of the sign with a suitable phase of the Moon to achieve a desired result. Some signs are for planting, some for cultivation, and still others for irrigation or even destruction.

All of this talk of cycles brings to mind the first chapter of the Bible:

> And God said, Let there be lights in the firmament of the heaven to divide the day from the night; and let them be for signs, and for seasons, and for days, and for years:
>
> And let them be for lights in the firmament of the heaven to give light upon the earth: and it was so.
>
> And God made two great lights; the greater light to rule the day, and the lesser light to rule the night: and he made the stars also. (Genesis 1:14-16)

This quote is from the King James version, but, while Bibles may vary in wording, they all have essentially the same meaning.

We have no intention of trying to interpret the Bible – not even three verses of it – but it is apparent that what is being conveyed in these verses, the cycles referred to, are very much what this book is about.

The "greater light" is, of course, the Sun. No single book could even attempt to explain the multitude of influences the Sun has on the earth and on all living things, plant and animal.

The "lesser light" is the Moon, and this book is concerned with the

28-day-plus cycle of the Moon, and the influence it has over living things, both plant and animal. We don't claim that it covers all of the Moon's spheres of influence. That, too, could never be done in one book or, we suspect, in one lifetime.

We are concerned here with the "lesser light" and its cycle. We are concerned with two sets of conditions that arise during this cycle: the phase, which is determined by the time when the Moon's journey brings it to each of the four quadrants of the sky; and the signs, determined by the Moon's passage through that segment of the heavens where other stars' (planets') influences are strongest.

As you work with this book, the nature of the Moon's journey becomes increasingly clear. You will be able to combine the sign with the Moon phase to achieve whatever your aim might be. There is wide latitude. No one way is absolutely right. You will always have a choice, so you can tailor the task to your available time.

At first you might say, "My aim is production; I want to grow vegetables and fruits in profusion." This is a perfectly natural and good aim, but it is not the only aim for every gardening project.

As an example of how varied your aims might be, take the case of planting a shade tree. We know that Cancer is a fruitful, moist and productive sign. Combined with the 2nd Quarter of the Moon, it would be a wonderful time for planting seeds for future tomato plants.

But if you contemplate planting a shade tree, Cancer might be too productive, causing too much growth, a top-heavy tree requiring constant cropping to keep it from being uprooted by the first windstorm. So, in the case of the shade tree, you might choose the 3rd Quarter of the Moon (since a tree is a perennial, depending on its rootstock for survival through the seasons and through the years). And you might wish to consider the sign of Taurus, known for producing good roots and sturdy trunks or stems. It's a question of choosing a sign that suits your purpose and a Moon phase that will abet your task.

Nature follows cycles. And we are concerned with the cycle of the Moon. As you plant, as you reap, as you live your daily life, working with the energies of this continuing cycle will make the task easier. Using the Moon's phase and sign as you plant a shade tree is following nature's way of helping you to successfully complete the job.

In the charts in this book (as well as from other sources) you will find that Cancer is generally conceded to be the most productive sign, followed by Scorpio and Pisces. But you have a wide choice of suitable signs for planting. Each sign, by its nature, has certain qualities that are more desirable than others for specific tasks.

When you plant by the Moon's phases and signs, you have wide latitude, a variety of possible combinations, therefore, a choice of suitable times. It is true that you are not as free as you might be if you planted whenever the whim arises, but is this harum-scarum approach what you really want for gardening, or for living? We think not. Gardening is a discipline; you are joining forces with the cycles of nature. You are planting to produce specific results based on your knowledge of these natural cycles, whether that be bushels of red ripe tomatoes ready for canning, or a sturdy shade tree for the west wall of your home, with its roots, trunk and branches in perfect proportion.

There is another aspect here that most gardeners overlook, even those who have long planted by "the signs," and who are adept at this kind of gardening. If the New Moon occurs in a fruitful sign, the entire 28-day lunar cycle will be more fruitful than if the New Moon occurs in a barren sign, and vice versa.

For example: If the New Moon in this particular month occurs in Scorpio, a watery and fruitful sign, you know that Scorpio will produce good, healthy vine growth – that is the nature of the sign. So, what you have for the 28-day lunar cycle is a kind of Scorpio "overlay," as it were. For the entire lunar month, through all phases and in all signs, this fruitful overlay will be present, adding the extra element of good vine growth. This overlay influence can work for you or work against you, depending on the project at hand, but with the knowledge that it exists, you are prepared, and you can cope with it.

Now, let's see how this is possible. Suppose, for example, you were planting tomatoes in the 2nd Quarter (the phase of the Moon for above-ground crops with seeds on the inside), and the day you were planting the Moon was in Pisces. In that case, the Scorpio New Moon overlay would only add an extra element of fruitfulness to the already-excellent sign of Pisces. Since the Moon phase and sign were perfect for tomatoes, and since you have a fruitful overlay, your planting should produce superior results.

Using the same example – the New Moon in Scorpio, giving a fruitful overlay to the entire cycle – if our task is to destroy, we must make a special effort to have all other aspects in our favor. We must overcome the fruitful overlay of Scorpio's influence for the 28-day cycle. Remember, our purpose is to destroy. We have a briar patch adjacent to our garden and we wish to lengthen our bean rows in that direction. We need to destroy the briars, no easy task. We know the 4th Quarter is the best Moon phase for destroying unwanted growth (the energy cycle is low), so we consult our almanac.

We find that we are fairly restricted as to barren signs available in this quarter. With the New Moon in Scorpio, we find that Virgo, Libra, Scorpio and early degrees of Sagittarius are possible signs for our briar-killing job. In this instance, we have only two good choices: Virgo and Sagittarius, both barren signs, and since we have only certain degrees (hours) of Sagittarius, we will choose Virgo, the most barren choice – giving us a full two-and-a-half-day period for the work.

Since we are destroying in a good Moon phase, the 4th Quarter, and since we are destroying the briars in the sign of Virgo, a barren sign, we will have adequately overcome the fruitful overlay of Scorpio. We have two strong aspects going for us – the Moon phase and the barren sign – and we will be able to destroy the briars.

We have explained how these overlays come about, through the nature of the sign on the first day of the lunar cycle, the New Moon. It is now time we review all the available overlays that could occur with each New Moon, each lunar cycle, so we will know what to expect from all twelve signs.

If the New Moon occurs in a water sign (Cancer, Scorpio or Pisces) you will have a fertile overlay for that cycle. If the New Moon occurs in an earth sign (Taurus or Capricorn, with Virgo being discussed separately because it presents other problems), you have an overlay good for root crops or for bulbs and perennials.

Remember, too, that each earth sign tends to produce more foliage than fruit, so be sure you keep this aspect of the nature of earth signs in mind. Any one of five signs (Cancer, Scorpio, Pisces, Taurus and Capricorn) falling on a New Moon will produce an overlay that will encourage growth.

The fire signs – Leo, Sagittarius and Aries, will produce a barren overlay when any of them fall on the first day of the New Moon. It would make the entire 28-day lunar cycle that much more difficult for producing, or that much easier for destroying. The air signs – Gemini and Aquarius, but not Libra, will produce a barren overlay.

As you can readily see, both Virgo and Libra are exceptions. Virgo is an earth sign. At first blush you might assume that it is a fruitful sign. By now you know that Virgo is barren, even though it is both a feminine and an earth sign. Virgo may be used for foliage growth, but never for fruit production. For a shrub, yes; for a tomato, never.

Now, conversely, Libra is a masculine air sign. Logic would lead you to believe, therefore, that it would be poor for planting. Yet, you know from earlier chapters that it is semi-moist. You know that because of its Venus rulership; it is good for some types of planting, and it is especially good for the planting of flowers – for beauty, for aroma, for rarity. Keep this in mind: Libra will produce great beauty; it will produce the rare and exotic, BUT this is not a fruitful sign, so it will not produce without work. You will have to be willing to invest time in the care of your flowers, and you will have to work for Libra's beauty. They may have to be sprayed and they may have to be watered and fertilized. They will need care, but the results will be worth it.

Now, if either Libra or Virgo are the signs on the first day of the lunar cycle (New Moon), they will produce an overlay that is individualistic, something that will not apply specifically to either air or earth, but something that is individual to the nature of these two signs. Libra, for example, would tend to help with your efforts to plant as long as you chose a good phase and a good sign for the job at hand. Virgo would produce an overlay that would tend to impede your efforts, for Virgo is barren. She will make foliage for you; she will not produce for you. Virgo is the sign of the virgin, not the mother.

That explains the theory of the overlay, the influence, that comes from the nature of the sign on the day of the New Moon, an influence that will last through the 28-day-plus cycle. This is an influence only; it is not the strongest factor. It is something to be aware of, something to use; but, your first job is to find the correct phase of the Moon, and the second is to choose a sign that fits with the job at hand. All other considerations, including this overlay factor, are secondary.

We have friends who are amused by our avid interest in planting by the Moon phases and signs. We are often the butt of little jokes. Yet we are able to provide them with the fruits of our labors, the excess over our needs, from our "Moon-cycle-oriented" garden.

We certainly didn't invent the system, and we don't claim that all the ideas in this book are ours. What we have attempted to do is bring together all the information available so that there will be a ready reference for the new gardener, or even the old one who is open-minded enough to use the lore of his legion of ancestors.

We readily agree that for a long time planting by the signs and the phases of the Moon was given too little credence in many quarters. But, in recent years, scientists who are interested in provable facts have begun to come to some interesting conclusions based on their own controlled studies, based on the provable evidence they are able to produce. Some of these experiments have been cited throughout this book. And, because they are all based on cycles, we will mention a few more.

In a study in France, E. Graviou accurately and scientifically measured the oxygen uptake of seeds during the lunar phases, and he said, in part: "... there is a lunar synchronization of biological material and atmospheric pressure." Scientists talk "funny." Maybe it is to impress each other, for he could have said the same thing much more simply: "... the Moon is the timer, the controller, of all living things on earth, and of the atmosphere in which they live."

Mr. E. Graviou is so right. The cycles of the Moon affect our weather, our water, and all living organisms. The purpose of this book is to show how some of the "synchronization" that Graviou speaks of came about.

Dr. Jane J. Panzer of Tulane University found, in her studies, that seeds were regulated in their water uptake, and thus in their germination, and that this regulation was based on lunar cycles. "Water uptake peaked at every quarter Moon, and was especially marked approaching Full Moon," she said. "In fact, seeds took in twice as much water on the Full Moon as at other times in the monthly cycle."

There are many examples of scientific studies that bear out the conclusions in this book. We do not claim the information we have on every line and every page has been scientifically proven. In our opinion, there is still too little interest by the scientific community, but we welcome the fact that there is increasing interest in investigating the lore of Moon planting. We are also happy that chicken soup – "Mama's cold remedy"—has finally been vindicated, and that "an apple a day" has achieved scientific status. We are glad to see studies being done that prove the efficacy of some of the herbal treatments once so extensively used, but which have fallen from favor as "modern" medicine has evolved. All these studies tend to support the wisdom of our forebears, and it is refreshing to know that brains were not "invented" in the 20th Century.

There have been articles in recent years concerning the "biological clocks." Scientific research has proven that these mechanisms exist – both in people and in plant life – but science is not yet able to explain the "whys" of this phenomenon. Dr. Steven M. Reppert and Dr. William J. Schwartz, both of Massachusetts General Hospital and Harvard Medical School, have conducted a study of the biological clock in unborn rats. It was published in 1983 in the Journal of Science. Read the article. This is not lore; it is late-20th Century science.

All plants and animals have this biological clock. You do, too. It can be upset by jet travel; many different things can throw it out of focus. Doctors sometimes term it a "disturbance in the sleep pattern." It is a serious thing when the biological clock is malfunctioning in a human being. It requires specialized treatment, which is becoming more available because so much is being learned about the biological clock.

The point is, cycles control our lives more than we realize. We are looking at only one set of cycles, the cycle of the Moon. The entire theme of this book has been the twenty-eight-day-plus cycle of the Moon as it passes through its various phases and signs, providing periods of growth or rest, moisture or lack of moisture.

In your garden or in your life, make nature your ally, not your adversary. Your understanding of the Moon's cycles is a way to work with your ally.

Chapter 12

Fishing

If we were able to give you one simple rule for good fishing, we would earn the everlasting goodwill of the world's anglers – all of them, without exception.

Unfortunately, however, there are almost as many theories as there are fishermen. (And almost as many fish tales, too.)

Our purpose in this chapter is to outline several theories, most of which are based on the Moon's phase or sign, or a combination of these, along with the Sun, Sun speed, or the speed of the Moon.

In each instance we will give The Rule as it applies to that theory, and then we will amplify it with the reasons behind it.

In this chapter we will cover: Moon Signs for the best fishing; Phases of the Moon, as they apply to fishing specifically; Choosing Fishing Hours, the How and the Why; Tides; Barometer; and, Temperatures, both of the water and air.

Moon Signs

THE RULE: Fish when the Moon is in any of the three water signs: Pisces, Cancer or Scorpio, and in that order. If none of these are feasible, try Aquarius, Gemini, Libra, Capricorn, Virgo and Taurus, in descending order. Skip the three fire signs.

In an extensive analysis of good fishing days, Pisces, the sign of the fishes, leads the list. Fishing while the Moon is in this sign will give you the most favorable conditions. This will be lessened only when the Moon is at its lowest energy flow, i.e., when Pisces falls in the last three days of the Old Moon or the first two days of the New Moon, before the energies have had time to manifest.

However, even if Pisces falls in this debilitated phase of the Moon, you will still find fishing to be good, although not the best. So, Pisces is definitely the No. 1 Moon sign choice for fishing.

The second most powerful water sign to ensure good fishing is Cancer, the sign most readily identified with the Moon. There is a natural affinity here. Use it. Fishing conditions when the Moon is in Cancer will be excellent, too, but keep in mind the period of time when the Moon's energies are at low ebb – three days before the New Moon and two days after. In this period, just as with Pisces, excellent fishing will be down-graded by this dearth of energy. Instead of "best," it will be "good."

So you see, Pisces and Cancer are both excellent signs; both have the same strengths and weaknesses. Cancer, for fishing, is slightly less strong, and perhaps this is because it is preceded by a fairly weak fishing sign (Gemini), and followed by Leo, which is downright poor. Pisces, on the other hand, is preceded by Aquarius, one of the four big ones, and followed by Aries, a poor sign, but better by far than Leo. Perhaps this is the reason; perhaps it isn't.

As mentioned, Scorpio and Aquarius are both good, even excellent, fishing signs when given the powers of an energized Moon. Scorpio is third choice over Aquarius, but only by a small margin.

But even the worst signs for fishing can be lifted by the energies of a growing Moon, or even by a waning Moon that has not lost too much of its power. The three days following the Full Moon would still have useful energy.

So, if you want a good Moon sign for fishing, here they are in declining order: Pisces, Cancer, Scorpio, Aquarius, Gemini, Libra, Capricorn, Virgo and Taurus. Except for an outing on the lake, a picnic or water skiing, forget about the three fire signs. They are, in our opinion, in descending order of value: Aries, Sagittarius, and, lastly, Leo.

We feel it is valid to say that fishing is improved when the Moon is growing in strength, but this simple rule overlooks those excellent fishing days immediately following a Full Moon. If you were to discount those three to four days, you'd anger an army of true-believers.

We want to stress the point that the first two days of a New Moon can debilitate, or at least mitigate, an otherwise strong fishing sign, because the Moon has not yet grown sufficiently to fully power those signs. Keep it in mind.

Now, let's talk about the Full Moon itself. Here is where you can really get into an argument with almost every fisherman who pays any attention to fishing's natural pluses and minuses. There are those who will say firmly: "All Full Moons are good, regardless of the sign," and those who say, "Full Moons are good, especially if they occur in any water sign." And then there are those who believe, "The best day of any month is the day after a Full Moon." This always creates a chorus of, "That's a good day, but the day of the Full Moon is always better."

Additionally, there are avid fishermen who don't want to be restricted by the 28-day Full Moon cycle. These anglers will say, "Not just a Full Moon, but any day when the Moon is changing quarters is a good fishing day. If you don't believe it, try it."

Now, what do we say to all of this? Who is right?

All of them can be right, given the right set of conditions. Weather is a factor, and this would include a steady or rising barometer; the water temperatures and air temperatures are also to be reckoned with; the Moon South most certainly is a factor (see Choosing Fishing Hours, a subsection of this chapter); water conditions, whether clear or roiled; and, of course, the time of day. If all of these external conditions are just right, you could have good fishing in even a bad sign and a poor Moon phase.

But fishing is an art. There is a skill that goes beyond the use of a rod and reel and the correct choice of a lure. That skill is the bringing together of all the possible advantages on any given day, or in choosing a day that has several (and the more the better) of these positive factors.

Choosing a good fishing sign is one of these factors. So is choosing a good phase of the Moon. And then, the choice of the fishing hours cannot be discounted.

The Moon's phase, we believe, is far less important than sign, but it is a plus factor, so our thumbnail phase advice would be: "Fish any time in the lunar month except five days before and two days after a New Moon." In this way you get a growing strength, or a Moon whose energies are still high, even if waning day by day.

Before we leave this section on the Moon's phases, let's talk about fishing in daylight hours or at night.

It is almost axiomatic that fishing in the morning or evening hours, especially in summer, is productive, so we will not dwell on it. Fishing at dawn or dusk is so universally recommended that we won't try to gild the lily.

As to day and night fishing hours, one theory is that when there is a bright Moon, fish can see to feed at night, and therefore, are not so hungry in the daylight hours. If this is true, then fishing on moonlight nights would prove productive. Conversely, in the dark of the Moon, you would find more fish during daylight hours because of their "restricted" nighttime feeding.

Our Opinion: An interesting theory, but we were unable to find any real evidence to support it. That is not to say that it isn't valid; it is just that our research is inconclusive.

We did find fishing calendars that are based entirely on this one idea. These calendars give the *best* night fishing as three days before the Full Moon and three days after; *good* night fishing days were the seven to eight days preceding and following these seven days of *best* fishing; and the *poor* night fishing days were the three days before the New Moon, the day of its occurrence, and the three days following it.

The *best* daytime fishing, of course, was the exact opposite of this, the seven days that include the New Moon with three days before and three days after. The *good* days for daylight fishing were the seven or eight days that precede and follow these *best* fishing days; and the *poor* daylight fishing days were the three days before and after the Full Moon.

Using this theory, if you take a calendar page and ink in the *best* days and the *good* days, both night and day, you will find that you have seven *best* days each for both night *and* day fishing, and sixteen or seventeen days that are good for either night or day fishing. There are no poor days – only poor choices of daylight hours or darkness.

We leave judgment on this to you. If you like it, and if it works for you, then use it. As we have indicated, there are such fishing calendars available.

Remember, fishing calendars or fishing booklets listing *best, good, fair* and *poor* fishing days are on the market because they sell. We have looked at a number of them; we have analyzed them, checked them by sign and by phase. Some of them are extremely simplistic. We hope this chapter will give you sufficient information for making a suitable choice if you should decide to use such a calendar or booklet.

Choosing Fishing Hours

THE RULE: Fish one hour before and one hour after the time of a Moon South, or at an hour approximately twelve-and-a-half hours hence. For a shorter period and to a lesser degree, fish approximately six-and-a-quarter hours before or six hours after a Moon South.

Now, there's a real mouthful that must have an explanation. A "Moon South" is that hour when the Moon is directly overhead in your time zone or in the time zone where you are fishing. It will occur at Noon on a New Moon and at midnight on a Full Moon. Yes, we are fully aware that the Moon can be directly overhead only if you live at or on the equator, but when we say directly overhead, we mean that the Moon is at its highest point in the heavens for your area. On each day following the New Moon, that Moon position, or the hour it is directly overhead, will be altered slightly as it moves from Noon to Midnight, just fourteen to fifteen days later.

As an example: The Moon could be directly overhead at 12 Noon on the day of the New Moon, and then at 12:45 p.m. the next day, at 1:30 the third day, 2:02 the fourth, and so on, until on the day of the Full Moon it would be directly overhead at midnight. Remember, this is just an example, for the time change from day to day will vary, depending on the hour of moonrise and moonset, which we will go into later in this chapter.

The hour when the Moon is directly overhead, whether or not it is visible, is called a Moon South, and a Moon South signals a prime period for fishing. This prime period can last for two to two-and-a-half hours and will begin about an hour and fifteen minutes before the Moon South and continue until one hour and fifteen minutes after it. There are two such periods: one occurs at the hour when the Moon South occurs – when the Moon, in your location, is directly above the earth – and the other is twelve-and-a-half hours later, when the Moon is directly below the earth, but still in line with the Sun.

To repeat, there are two prime fishing periods. There are, also, two of what might be called "secondary" periods. These two secondary periods occur approximately six-and-a-quarter hours before and six-and-a-quarter hours after the hour of the Moon South, but allow only about an hour to an hour-and-a-half for best fishing results. So, you would start fishing thirty to forty-five minutes before the determined secondary hour, and fish for forty-five minutes after it.

"Great information," you say. "There are two days each month – New Moon and Full Moon – when I will know the hours when fishing will be most productive. What about these other days in the lunar cycle?" You're right, of course. It's time for an explanation of how you can determine the hour of the Moon South on any day of any month or year.

Moon South is shown in some almanacs, but not in all. The hour of the Moon's rise and the hour of its setting is commonly given. This is standard information, readily available, even if you don't have an almanac indicating Moon South. Check your daily paper's weather column. Moonrise and moonset are usually listed there, as are the times of the Sun's rise and set. If this is not the case, call your local weather bureau. They can give you this information on a weekly, monthly or even yearly basis.

Once you have the time of the moonrise and moonset for any given day, you determine the hours and minutes between rise and set, and then divide this by two and add it to the Moonrise time. The answer is the hour of Moon South for your time zone (or fishing area).

For clarity, let's take an example. Suppose you know that the moonrise is 6:39 a.m. in your time zone, and that the Moon set is 9:53 p.m. It will take 5 hours 21 minutes to get to the hour of Noon, and then another 9 hours 53 minutes to get to the time the Moon sets, a total of 15 hours and 14 minutes. You divide this in half, which gives you 7 hours and 37 minutes. When you add this figure to the hour the Moon rises, you get 2:16 p.m. That, for the day shown in this example, is the time of the Moon South. (6:39 a.m. plus 7:37 equals 14:16 or 2:16 p.m.)

Now, you know how to determine a Moon South in your area for any day or any year. From this one key time, you can determine the other prime fishing time, plus the two secondary fishing times for the day.

Earlier we said that the second prime fishing time was when the Moon was directly below the earth, approximately twelve-and-a-half hours later. That "approximately" is bothersome, but man's method of keeping time is not always entirely in harmony with nature. Simple evidence of this is leap year, when we gain a day every four years in our attempt to make our method of timekeeping at least workable, and so it is with this "approximate" twelve-and-a-half hours to be added. Twelve hours may be exactly half of one of our days, but it is not half of a lunar day. While the exact figure will vary from day to day, for all practical purposes you can add twelve hours and twenty-five minutes to the time of Moon South and you will achieve a workable hour for your second prime period for fishing.

Remember, these prime periods, both the Moon South and the one you compute, are the center of the prime periods. Begin your fishing at least an hour to an hour-and-a-half ahead, and fish for an hour or more after.

Now, if you use the twelve hours twenty-five minutes for determining the second prime period, what figure will you use for the "secondary" periods, those that are "approximately six-and-a-quarter hours before or after the hour of Moon South"? This, too, will vary slightly, but this will work: Subtract six hours and twelve minutes for the one preceding the time of Moon South, or add it, to determine the time for the period following Moon South.

Does this all sound too complex? It really isn't, but if computing doesn't appeal to you, find a calendar or almanac that shows Moon South for your time zone. Then with the simple addition of 6:12, 12:25, and the subtraction of 6:12 minutes from that Moon South time, you have the peak of each of the four best fishing periods in that day.

If this is too complex, if you don't want to do any computing, be assured that someone has done it for you. Many newspapers and TV stations subscribe to a service that provides these fishing periods. There are several available services, but the best known is the Solunar Tables as devised by the late John Alden Knight. If neither your newspaper nor TV station carries these tables, you can write for a booklet containing all the hours for every day of the year. It is published by Mrs. Richard Alden Knight, Box 207, Montoursville, PA 17754, priced at $2.00, or was the last time we purchased a copy.

Our methods for determining Moon South and what we call prime or secondary good fishing periods are not necessarily the methods devised by Mr. Knight many years ago. We do not pretend to know Mr. Knight's methods, but we do know his work was based on the time of the occurrence of Moon South. We also know that fishing at these prime and secondary periods will produce results. These are the times when fish (and animals) tend to feed on a given day.

Tides

THE RULE: Fishing is best at one hour before and one hour after high tide; one hour before and one hour after low tide.

Very simply stated, that is the rule for fishing hours based on the tides if you happen to live at or near the seaside. If you are familiar with fishing and tides in your area, you could enlarge upon this rule, based on your experience.

However, fishing is usually better on a high tide than on a low tide. In each instance you are looking for that period of time just before and just after a tide change. Generally, but not always, there are two high tides and two low tides each day – four periods in each twenty-four hours – when the fishing is especially good. High tides are longer and better fishing times than low tides.

Now, doesn't this all begin to sound familiar? Two prime periods each day and two secondary periods. Of course it does. The reason it sounds so familiar is that there is a common denominator. The fresh water fisherman is interested in the Moon South; the salt water fisherman in high tide. The common denominator for both is the Moon, the daily lunar cycle.

Moon South is that time of day or night in any particular area when the Moon, whether visible or not, is directly overhead; one of the high tides is that time of day or night in any particular area when the Moon, whether visible or not, is directly overhead. The second high tide, as is the case with the second of the prime fishing periods timed by Moon South, is that time of day or night when the Moon, whether visible or not, is directly below the earth.

In either case, whether for the two prime fishing periods or the two high tides, this is a period when the Earth, the Sun and the Moon are in direct line, each to the other.

Therefore, these two are not separate things; both occur at that time of day when you have a Moon South, or when the Moon is directly the opposite of Moon South. In fresh water, you have no indication of it, but in salt water you have tides, visible proof of the Moon's effect on the earth.

Those secondary fishing periods, those times that occur six-and-a-half hours before and six-and-a-half hours after the Moon South, do they have a tide equivalent? Of course they do. They are the two low tides, which are secondary periods of good fishing in salt water.

So, whether or not it is apparent, the Moon affects all the water on earth – fresh or salt. All good salt water fishermen are keenly aware of this, and fish with the action of the tides. They are tide-conscious, because they know this knowledge means the difference between a good catch and a "catch-as-catch-can" trip.

Some fresh water fishermen are aware of the Moon South and some use fishing tables based on it, but most of them are unaware of the tidal pull of the Moon on their fishing waters, and thereby lose the advantage of fishing when fish are feeding.

These periods of prime and secondary fishing are not haphazard events on fresh water or sea water. They are periods timed by the cycle of the Moon's daily journey, and keyed to that time of day when the Moon is directly overhead, directly underfoot, or at right angles to one of these positions.

These periods can be ascertained for any location on earth. Near the coast, all newspapers carry tidal information, so time your fishing to coincide with this data. Fresh water fishermen in the vicinity of the shore can also use the same tidal information. Those inland fishermen, without tidal information, can get Moon South information from their almanacs, or get moonrise-moonset information and make their own computations. For those who don't want to make this effort, try the Solunar Tables, or one of the other similar tables.

Now, before we move on, what about those of you who don't mind computing and who have already said, "Wait a minute now, I live in a wide state. My standard time zone is based on 75 degrees longitude, but I live in Asheville, NC, which is 82 degrees 33 minutes – many miles west of the 75-degree imaginary line. Don't tell me that Moon South information in an almanac that has been based on EST will be accurate for me."

We won't. We know there will be a variation within any time zone, depending on how far east or west of the standard meridian you may live. But, for all practical purposes, you can use the standard meridian and your fishing period won't be too far off.

If you are a stickler, if you must have your fishing periods more accurately pinpointed, here is the rule: Determine how many degrees you live east or west of the standard meridian, then multiply that difference by four minutes. Now you have the actual time variance from a quoted Standard meridian. If you live west of your Standard meridian, add this variance to the Moon South you have computed; if you live east of the

Standard meridian, subtract from your computed Moon South time.

For example, the location of Asheville, NC is 82 degrees and 33 minutes longitude. That would be seven-and-a-half degrees west of the Eastern Standard Time meridian of 75 degrees. If your computed Moon South was 8:35 p.m. EST, you would add 30 minutes, which is seven-and-a-half degrees times four minutes (or 30 minutes). You add it because you live west of the EST meridian used in the computation of the moonrise-moonset.

If you were to buy a yearly book of Solunar Tables, you would find a method of making minor corrections for this variation from your standard time meridian. In that booklet, for example, you use the fishing hours listed, but for North Carolina you subtract 15 minutes. This, obviously, is a compromise figure, or an "average" figure, that would fit most areas of the state. If you must be bone accurate, compute it for yourself at 4 minutes per degree of variation. In the case of Asheville, 30 minutes is far more correct than 15 minutes, but what is that amount of time to a fisherman? Patience is one of the virtues all fishermen learn early. (Those who don't either give up or get ulcers.) If the good fishing period begins at 2:30 p.m., he won't mind starting half an hour early, to be sure he's there when the action begins.

Barometer

THE RULE: Fish on a steady or rising barometer. Barometric pressures are easy to ascertain. Most of us have a barometer in our homes as a part of the weather wall plaque, although many notice only the temperature or humidity dials. Use the barometer, too. It is useful. Usually there is a little thumb-screw in the middle of the dial that controls a movable needle. Set this needle exactly on the present barometric pressure. This is another needle, one over which you have no control. Several hours later, look at the barometer. Is the barometric pressure indicator rising, falling, or holding steady? This will tell you a great deal.

A high barometric pressure reading, or one that is rising, will signal good weather or improving weather. Conversely, a low reading, or one that is falling, will signal bad or deteriorating weather conditions.

The average barometric pressure at sea level is 29.92, so anything above that would be considered high and anything below that would be considered low. It is important to know if the pressure is rising or falling, so don't overlook this indicator. That's the purpose in setting the movable needle on the instrument.

All living creatures are affected by barometric pressure, but that is only one factor in fishing. In bad weather the water is likely to be roiled, the surface rough, and the water – with abundant rain – can become silted or cloudy, even downright muddy. These conditions are not ideal for fishing.

As the barometer rises and the weather begins to clear, conditions return to normal, and the fish – who may not have been feeding during these unsatisfactory conditions – begin to move in search of food.

At this point you may be saying, "Fine, all very interesting. The barometer might affect fishing, but does it belong in a book about the Moon's phases and signs?" Yes, it does. We know our weather is affected by the Moon; the waters of the earth feel the effects, and both water and weather conditions are prime factors in fishing. The relationship is more complex than can be gone into in the context of this book, but it is real all the same.

For the purpose of choosing a good day for fishing, an explanation is really not needed. Simply use your barometer as one of several considerations that you will be making.

Let's make a quick review:

Rising Pressure – Clearing, improving weather.
High Pressure – Clear days or days without rain.
Falling Pressure – Deteriorating weather
Low Pressure – Stormy, rainy, windy.

Temperature

THE RULE: Fish the depth at which the water is the temperature suitable for the species sought.

That doesn't help much, does it? There is nothing really specific there, and for good reason. There can be no hard and fast rule for all fish. Each variety has its own temperature comfort range. Where possible, each species will seek the water level that gives them their own specific "comfort zone."

Smallmouth bass, for example, prefer waters that range from 60 to 70 degrees Fahrenheit, and will leave waters that approach the 90-degree mark. On the other hand, anything below 60 degrees Fahrenheit is not to their liking, either. Outside air temperatures, sunny days, cause smallmouth to move about, seeking that comfortable layer of water, which may be near the surface or well below it.

Largemouth bass, on the other hand, prefer warmer water than their smallmouth cousins. They will spawn when temperatures are as low as 62 to 64 degrees Fahrenheit. Hatching can occur at 62 to 64 degrees, but the time will be cut in half by a water temperature of 80 degrees. Look for this species in warmer waters. On very hot, sunny days, look for them under the shade of a weedbed.

As another example, muskellunge feed best in water that is about 68 degrees, and they will stop eating altogether if the water temperature approaches 90 degrees. Spawning for the muskellunge won't occur until water temperatures reach at least the 48- to 56-degree level.

The point is, each species, and sometimes each sub-species, has its own "comfort level," and will find this stratum. (Water tends to lie in layers by temperature.) If you want strikes (and who doesn't?), you must fish at the depths where the fish are, or you will end up with an empty creel.

So, for productive fishing, you need to know two things: One, the temperature the species prefer; and, two, the level in the body of water where that temperature can be found.

If you are to fish successfully, whatever the catch, you are going to have to know something about its feeding habits and habitat. Without this knowledge, you will just be casting blindly. So, along with the information you gather before you begin the fishing trip, make a note to find out what water temperatures your intended catch prefers, so you can put your lure at least in the area where it might be found. This will take a little research on your part, but it will be well worth the effort.

There are many books on the varieties of the world's fishes. One that we think is excellent is McClane's Standard Fishing Encyclopedia, published by Holt, Rinehart and Winston. This reference book, or any one of several others, will give you information on water temperature preferences, and even information on feeding habits and preferred habitats.

Once this information is ascertained, you will need to know where in the lake or stream the proper water temperature can be found. This, of course, will vary from season to season, even from day to day, depending on weather conditions.

The answer is a fishing thermometer. You can buy one or devise one. A fishing thermometer is attached to a line with a mark at each foot level. You lower and raise it, checking until you find the stratum of water with the desired temperature. Fish at that depth – at the level where the fish are likely to be found because of their comfort.

Yes, you'll find water temperature thermometers available, made specifically for fishing. They will vary in design and cost, but a good one will have a cup-like device so that you can sample water at a specified level, and bring it back up in water from that level, without distorting the temperature as it comes through the warmer upper levels of the lake.

There are many devices that can give the water temperature at various levels, from the simple to the sophisticated, and even from your own jury-rigged thermometers, but the principle is the same. You are looking for a stratum, a layer of water, where the temperature is to the liking of the species you have set out to catch.

Water does lie in layers, especially in the warmer period of the year. There are three main layers: The first, near the surface, tends to be warmer, and tends to fluctuate more radically, depending on weather conditions; the second one – and these vary in depth, depending on the terrain and the body of water – is thinner than the first, and generally ranges from 65 degrees at the bottom of the layer to 70 degrees at the top; the third, the largest and deepest layer, goes from about 45 to 65 degrees.

We recommend that you experiment with water temperature in your own favorite "fishing hole." Each body of water is individual; each tends to heat or cool in its own way, depending on many factors, but be assured that fishing will improve if you put your lure where the fish are, rather than expecting them to come to you.

So, what would make an ideal fishing day?

Let's start with a day just warm enough for your comfort, with the Moon in Pisces, in a period three days before or three days after a Full Moon, at an hour toward sunset when the Moon is directly overhead, when the barometer is both high and steady, and when the water temperature near the surface is between 60 and 70 degrees Fahrenheit, so we can use a topwater plug. Nothing to it!

We'd like to end this chapter with a quote, one of our favorite summations of the real value of fishing. This quote comes from a walnut paper weight, with a piece of silver anodized aluminum affixed to it, on which these words, anodized in blue, are written:

I pity any fellow who
Doesn't enjoy fishing.
Fishing, somehow, stimulates reflection,
Tempers the vicissitudes of business life,
Encourages contemplation,
Calms one's nerves.

Further, the Good Lord has ruled,
The time spent in fishing
And love-making
Shall not be detracted
From the life span of mortal man.
— Eugene T. Turney, Jr., President, Anodyne, Inc.

Chapter 13

So You Don't Believe? Experiments

You have an interest in planting by the signs or you wouldn't be reading this book. It has not been our goal to convert you; we simply included our experience and all the other information we could find concerning planting by the signs, and we tried to do it by category, so that it would be readily usable – if you are so inclined.

But we would like to point out that this "old wives tale" – along with many others – has been at least partially vindicated by the scientific community. These experiments with the growth of plants were not by the signs, per se. However, the facts seem to speak for themselves.

For example: At the University of Padua in Italy, Giovanni Abrami of the Department of Botany found in his experiments that the greatest growth in plant life occurred in spurts that peaked at 14.7 and 29.5 days. He said of these regular and repetitive occurrences, "... they appear to be best correlated with the phases of the New and Full Moon."

This is not an isolated event, for quite separate from Abrami's experiments, C. R. Karnick, in Poona, India, planted beds of licorice at varying times in the lunar cycle. His findings: The time of planting "affects the entire morphology, flowering and fruiting of plants."

So, unless you wish to discount the scientific experiments cited in this book – and there are many others – then you must conclude, at a minimum, that the Moon strongly affects more than just the tides. Truly, the Moon has a definite effect on fluids of all kinds: in the sea, in the soil – and in you. Blood, chemically, is quite similar to sea water. It's something to think about.

Let's assume you are NOT totally sold on gardening by Moon phases and signs, and let's further assume you need to tinker with these ideas, to try them out in small ways, before you give them a full effort in your own garden next Spring. If that is the case, here are a few minor experiments you might want to try:

Put a brick on some grass when the Moon is increasing, and watch the growing energy give sufficient life to the grass so that it will grow out from under the brick. Now put another brick in an adjacent spot on the same plot of grass during a decreasing (or waning) Moon, and watch the grass yellow and even die. If you try this you'll find, just as Abrami did in his experiments at the gardens of the University of Padua, that growth will occur in spurts (as the fruitful signs occur), peaking at Full Moon, and then peaking again at 29.5 days, which is just after the New Moon, when a new growth period begins.

Or, to put it another way, the energies of the period (New Moon to Full Moon) will permit growth under the brick, even when the plant is shielded from the benefits of the Sun. Blades of grass will find a way around the edges of the brick, as they reach toward the sun. But the grass under the brick, denied the energies of this growth period, will be sickly, yellowing, and may even die.

Another experiment is the digging of a post hole. Dig it in the light of the Moon (when digging will actually be easier), but wait to set your posts in the dark of the Moon. You will be rewarded with easier digging and a post that is firmly embedded. Now, reverse this procedure with another post. Dig in the dark of the Moon and set the post in the light of the Moon. Compare the two posts. The latter will have been harder to dig and the post will be less firmly embedded.

In the preceding paragraph did you note the parenthetical remark that in the light of the Moon "digging will actually be easier"? This may sound paradoxical, but it's true. Nothing in nature is static; it is all in motion. In the first two quarters of the Moon there is a period of expansion; conversely, the last two quarters are a period of contraction. Thus, digging in the light of the Moon is an easier job, and setting the posts in the dark of the Moon takes advantage of nature's contractions, so the dirt is contracted, tightened, around the post, and it stays more firmly in place.

Along the same lines, if you dig a hole in the light of the Moon, save the dirt and then try to refill that hole in the dark of the Moon, you will have more dirt than required. Try digging another hole in the dark of the Moon, and you will not have enough dirt to refill it. The reasons for this are exactly as has been cited several times in several ways: New Moon to Full Moon is a time of growing energy, of expansion;

Full Moon to the next New Moon is a time of declining energy and contraction.

And here is still another experiment with the expansion-contraction phenomenon. Have you ever noticed what happens when a board has been tossed outside on the ground? In some instances, over a period of time, you will find that board buried flush with the ground; in other instances the board will lie above ground, no matter how long it is allowed to stay there. The reason for this goes back to when the board was thrown there. If it's tossed out, or just laid on the ground to form a makeshift walkway, during the period of the Moon's expansion (New to Full), it will forever stay above ground. If it's placed there during the declining energy period, during the contraction, it will eventually settle into the ground until it becomes flush with the earth that surrounds it. It's not a major experiment, so give it try.

How about another one? You are already a gardener, or potential gardener, or you wouldn't have shown an interest in this book. Try a little gardening experiment. Choose any seed you are planning to plant, and give this a try. As an example, we'll use okra, so we'll know the kind of vegetable and, therefore, which phase and sign would be best for it.

For this experiment forget the most advantageous sign, and find a fruitful sign followed by a barren sign. Cancer and Leo will suit our purposes nicely. And, since okra is a vegetable with the seed on the inside, we will use the 2nd Quarter of the Moon, preferably close to the Full Moon, so there will be the smallest amount of time between the two plantings that you are going to make.

Plant the first seeds in the growing 2nd Quarter of the Moon in Cancer; plant the second batch with the Moon in the 3rd Quarter (just past Full) in the barren sign of Leo. You have a total period of approximately five days (two-and-a-half days for each sign, Cancer and Leo), so you should be able to span the plantings from the 2nd Quarter to the 3rd Quarter. (The soil and nutritional conditions should be about the same.)

Now, wait for the growth, fruiting, and production of these two plots of okra. You are doing your own experiment, although perhaps not under such stringent conditions as a scientist might. But, all the same, you have made an experiment under conditions that satisfy you. We are sure you will be willing to stand by the result. We think it will be an eye-opener.

Chapter 14

Miscellany

In this chapter – as was the case with Elsewhere Around the Homestead – we will be dealing with a variety of subjects. Because of the differences in subject matter, each must be dealt with as a separate entity.

THE RULE: Here again, one single rule cannot cover all of these diverse subjects. Each subheading in this chapter will be followed by the rule that applies to it. With that said, here is an alphabetical listing of the subjects: Acquisitions (Farmlands, Speculative Land, A Home, Livestock and Personal Items); Dental Care; Habits – How to Make or Break Them; Hair Care; Lawncare; Painting; Surgery; and Vision.

Acquisitions

(Under this category the rule varies slightly from section to section, so each will be dealt with individually.)

Buying a Farm, Additional Farmland, or a Home
THE RULE: Sign the contract for this type of permanent purchase on a New Moon (1st Quarter), or at least during a growing Moon (1st or 2nd Quarter), in one of the fixed signs: Taurus, Scorpio, Leo or Aquarius; otherwise, make the purchase when the Moon is in Capricorn.

That is the basic rule for such a purpose, but we have never asked you to blindly follow any phase or Moon sign. We have tried to tell you why these phases and signs are favored. So, why a New Moon, or at least a growing Moon – the 1st and 2nd Quarters of the Moon's 28-day cycle?

There are a couple of reasons: First, you're beginning something new: a new farm, new acreage, or a new home. These are challenges. Second, sign your paperwork as early as possible in a New Moon, when the energies are high, when you are in a period of growth. You'll need this energy. However perfect the farm may appear, it will still present challenges. It is new to you; you must learn about the soil, the water, the terrain. If you are a farmer, I needn't tell you that you must feel "at home" with your land or else you will not understand it and be able to extract the best from it.

A new house, new to you – no matter how new or old it may be – is a challenge. You won't know the house until you have lived in it, until you have experienced it. You are going to need the energies of an early growing Moon. This adjustment, at best, is rarely easy.

Farm land or a house may be picture-perfect on first inspection, but do not be deceived by appearances. This is a kind of "marriage contract" you have signed, and there will have to be considerable adjustments made. So be sure to have the energy of the New or growing Moon.

The sign is important, too. This is a purchase with an element of permanence to it, so be sure you select a fixed sign to augment the permanent nature of your purpose. We favor Taurus. It is a fixed sign, it favors acquisitions and is a semi-fruitful earth sign. Scorpio is an excellent second choice because it, too, is fixed, fruitful, and gives a strong, rugged growth to the project. Leo and Aquarius are both good because they are fixed by nature, and will bring the quality of steadfastness to the farmstead or to the new home acquired under this fixed influence.

Finally, there is Capricorn. This is not a "last choice," as it might appear, because Capricorn is the sign that governs business. Buying a farm or house under this sign would make the approach to the purchase more businesslike, more mature. Why is this? Because Capricorn is an earth sign (practicality); it is semi-fruitful (adding growth to the project); and, it is a Cardinal sign (dynamism).

Buying Acreage or a Home for Speculation

THE RULE: Sign your contracts in a waning Moon, preferably the 4th Quarter, with the Moon passing through any of the following: Capricorn, Cancer, Libra or Aries. Taurus may also be used as a fifth choice.

Now, why the waning Moon? Because you are not looking for the energy required for the "long haul" of running and maintaining a farm. This is not a permanent purchase, not meant to be lasting. You are looking for a profitable turnover. You are not building a family dynasty, a heritage. The waning Moon gives impetus to the short nature of this purchase.

Choose a time when the Moon is passing through one of the movable signs: Capricorn, Cancer, Libra or Aries, because of the transient nature of your purpose in making the purchase. You are buying for speculation – to keep for awhile and then sell at a profit.

These movable signs are listed in the order of their effectiveness. Capricorn must be first choice. It rules business and speculation and, of course, this is a business venture. It is an earth sign, which lends practicality; and it is a Cardinal-movable sign, which brings a dynamic rather than stagnant quality to the venture. Let us not forget that Capricorn is a semi-fruitful sign, a growth sign; and a speculative purchase is one that, by intent, is made for the purpose of growth of your investment.

Cancer is the second choice. It is a fruitful, growth sign. It will augment the speculative idea behind the purchase.

Libra is recommended especially if the purpose is to buy a rundown property to restore and then resell. As with flowers, Libra is the choice for beauty, and if you want to bring a house or a farm back to its peak condition, beauty is most certainly one of the prime factors.

Aries is favored because of the energy it generates. Aries won't allow you to sit on dead center wondering what to do; it will have you out selling the property.

The last sign is Taurus. This is a good one because it is semi-fruitful and a "practical" earth sign, but watch out for the fixed quality it possesses. Remember, Taurus is a collector, so the speculative purchase could turn into something you might want to keep. In short, a purchase under Taurus could start out as a speculation and end up as a possession.

Buying Livestock
THE RULE: Buy on, or just following, a New Moon when possible, or at least in a growing Moon (1st or 2nd Quarter), under the signs of Aquarius, Capricorn, Taurus, Libra or the fruitful signs of Cancer, Scorpio or Pisces.

When you add to your livestock you are adding new blood. It is the beginning of another "growing" phase, and, as with all new projects, you start on a new or at least a growing Moon, so that the energy of this phase of the Moon's cycle will bring expansion.

The Moon's sign, however, is a different thing altogether. Under ideal conditions, when you can time the purchase to fall under any sign of your choosing, you would select one that fits your purpose. For example: If you were buying a bull to improve the quality of your herd, or to breed a champion of your own, you might well time that purchase for the Moon's passage through Libra. This would add to your aim of producing offspring with beautiful conformation – real blue ribbon winners.

The purchase timing, however, is not as important as the timing of the breeding, but it is valid all the same. Your eye will be better able to see the true conformation, even if the bull you are buying is a young one.

Libra is far from the only choice you have. Remember, there are times when you have little choice in selecting the "perfect" Moon phase. But since you have a variety of good choices – seven signs – you can almost always make the purchase in a favorable sign.

Let's look at these seven signs individually to see what they do for our livestock purchase. No question about it, a New Moon in Aquarius is an ideal time to acquire new stock for your herd, or for starting a herd for the first time. By now you are fully aware of the energy of a New Moon, so that point won't be belabored. But why Aquarius? Aquarius, by the very nature of the sign, favors "new things," "new directions," "new ideas"; or, to put it another way, anything that points to the direction of or plans for the future. Aquarius is the "tomorrow" sign. When you are starting a herd, or adding to it, you are doing an Aquarian thing: You are building for tomorrow; you are building for the future. So you can see what a natural choice the growing New Moon really is when combined with the "growth for tomorrow" concept of Aquarius.

As we go through the rest of these signs, the Moon's phases (1st and 2nd Quarters) will not be repeated. Just assume that this fourteen-day period applies to all the other signs that follow under this subject heading.

Capricorn is a logical second choice. This earth sign (practicality) is ruled by Saturn, which brings permanence, sound business judgment, and over-all solidity to the whole venture. When you start or add to a herd you are making a business investment, so Capricorn is excellent.

Taurus (earth) is similar to Capricorn, in that it lends an element of practicality. Even though it doesn't have the business connotation that Capricorn has, it is the natural sign for acquiring, amassing, or collecting; for the building of an estate, or even for personal worth. You can readily see how this fits in with a herd. You are building, enlarging, improving your herd; you are adding to it for the purpose of personal financial growth – all very Taurian.

Libra has already been mentioned, and it is a perfectly serviceable sign, even if beauty is not the prime factor governing your purchase.

Now, lastly, the three fruitful signs: Cancer for abundance, Scorpio for good reproduction and sturdy offspring, and Pisces for the utilization of food and nutrients necessary for good growth.

Buying Personal Items
THE RULE: Buy during the 1st or 2nd Quarter, while the Moon is growing, and make that purchase during Taurus, Libra, Capricorn or Virgo.

A growing Moon phase is less important for personal items than it is for speculation, but we never want to buy anything if it's going to lose value. Why not use the energy of a growing Moon, especially when most personal purchases can be timed to suit individual requirements?

Taurus is the best choice for purchases of a personal nature: Taurus is the collector of "the things I need," or "the things I want." Primarily the latter.

Libra is good, too. Most of these personal purchases – jewelry, new clothes, a car – tend to be things where beauty is an important factor.

Capricorn is the sign which will add an element of practicality to personal purchases, so it will not only be something you want, but also something of value.

Capricorn also adds an element of tenacity. So whatever you buy, you will probably keep; or, if you sell, it will be for valid business reasons.

Finally, there's Virgo. Virgo has been kicked around a lot, hasn't it? Virgo, the Virgin, is barren, so it is used for nothing that requires reproduction, but it is picky, picky, picky. It is a detailist. It will want to see every facet of the "gemstone" you are considering; it will want to examine the mounting, consider the weight and even the salability of the purchase, should the necessity of selling occur. Virgo is persnickety, but isn't that a good thing when we are buying something personal, where we might be dazzled?

Before we leave Acquisitions in general, we hasten to say that we are well aware that we have not laid down rules for the purchase of every item that might cross your mind, but the idea is there. The rules that have been included can be interpolated, adjusted, and can be made to give the basis for choosing a good Moon phase and sign for any purchase.

As an example, what about an insurance policy? That's a far cry from anything that has been mentioned. What phase of the Moon and sign might be suitable for an insurance policy purchase?

First, it is something new, something just being started. You want the energy of a growing Moon, and so, ideally, you would choose the New Moon, or at least the 1st or 2nd Quarter.

Now, the sign: What is the purpose of the policy? To insure your crops (business), then Capricorn would be good; to insure your car or equipment (possessions), Taurus; or your health (solar plexus), Virgo.

So you see, with interpolation, and with the explanations that have gone before, you can make a wise decision both as to phase or sign.

Dental Care

THE RULE: For fillings, crowns, bridges or impressions, the 3rd and 4th Quarters of the Moon, in one of the fixed signs: Leo, Scorpio, Aquarius or Taurus. For extractions, or any kind of dental surgery, the 4th Quarter is the most desirable, followed by the 1st Quarter and, as a third choice, the 3rd Quarter, with the Moon in the signs of Gemini, Virgo, Sagittarius, Pisces or Capricorn.

In the instance of fillings, bridges or impressions, you are looking for a tight fit. You want these additions to your mouth to function at maximum efficiency and comfort. For that reason, the 3rd and 4th Quarters of the Moon are preferable, because this is the part of the Moon's cycle when energy is on the wane, when the tendency is to shrinkage rather than expansion. Consequently, work done at the time of the cycle's lowest energy ebb will fit. They will only tighten further when the energies expand. An impression for a plate, for example, if made when the gums are at their most compact, will be tight at the time of the impression, and will also fit, perhaps even tighter, as the Moon's energies expand.

The signs for fillings, bridges or impressions are the fixed signs of Leo, Scorpio, Aquarius and Taurus. Fixed signs, as the word implies, tend to be permanent, solid, unwavering. These fixed signs imply a bedrock, a foundation, and this is exactly what you want with fillings, bridges or impressions.

As we indicated, The Rule for extractions or any kind of dental surgery, differs from fillings, bridges and impressions. That is because of the difference in the nature of the dental work. Both extractions and dental surgery are more radical, and for that reason the 4th Quarter is preferable, and for two reasons: One, the Moon is at its lowest energy level, and two, because it is approaching its farthest distance from the Full Moon. Remember, when the Moon is full you are in a period when the body's fluids are under the greatest lunar influence, a time of expansion, therefore, excessive bleeding can be a real factor. (See the Surgery section of this chapter for additional detail.)

We cite the 1st Quarter as the second-most desirable quarter for extractions or dental surgery. Some people actually prefer this quarter. One of the reasons is that early in the phase, it is far removed from Full Moon, and it has the added advantage of being at the beginning of a period of rising energies, healing energies.

As stated in The Rule, the 3rd Quarter of the Moon may also be used, but is a lagging third choice. The later in the period the better, because of bleeding.

When it comes to choosing a sign for extractions or surgery, we recommend five signs, and not all for the same reasons. After you have looked them over, you may select one because of your own specific requirements. The key here is to understand what each sign offers to the process. As we explain why five signs are suitable, we will also explain why the other seven signs are less preferable.

The cycle of the Moon takes it through twelve signs in something over a twenty-eight-day period. These signs fall into three categories; Cardinal, Fixed and Mutable. Each of these categories has a quality attached to it. The four Cardinal signs tend to be active; the four Fixed signs resistant to change; and the four Mutable signs are negative, malleable or changeable – or perhaps "moldable" would better define it.

Since surgery in dentistry involves the area of the teeth, gums or mouth, Aries, ruling the head and upper teeth, would *not* be used. Always avoid the sign ruling the site of surgery.

The next sign, in order, is Taurus, ruling the lower teeth, jaw and throat. This, too, because of being the surgery site, or in proximity, should be avoided.

At this point we come to the first of the Mutable signs: Gemini. If you look at the numbered wheel that has been provided in the Glossary, you will see that both No. 1 and No. 2 (Aries and Taurus) have been eliminated as possibilities, so we are looking at No. 3, Gemini. If you choose to have your extractions in this Mutable (negative) sign, the Moon will pass through nine other signs before it returns to Aries, the site of extraction. (And, since it takes about two-and-a-half days to transit each, perhaps a little more, there are twenty-two days of healing before the energies of the Moon return to Aries, the operative site.) Gemini is an excellent sign for extractions or surgery.

Virgo is the second Mutable sign to consider, and it offers two advantages: One, it is the Mutable sign farthest from the site of surgery (in this case the mouth), and that is desirable; and, two, it rules the solar plexus and bowels, parts of the body far removed and with little or no connection to the surgical site.

The next Mutable sign as you move counter-clockwise around the wheel is Sagittarius. Its negative or moldable quality, plus its rulership over the liver and thighs, make it a good choice. It also has the advantage of being removed from the site of the extractions or surgery.

Pisces is the last of the mutable, and therefore negative, signs to be considered. Since the feet are exactly opposite the head on the human body, this might appear to be the most desirable sign for dental surgery, but it is not, and for a very good reason: The Moon travels counter-clockwise through the twelve signs, beginning with Aries and ending with Pisces. At this point, it begins a new cycle. Pisces, therefore, is but one sign removed from Aries, or one sign removed from the surgery site, allowing little time for healing before the Moon once again enters the affected area. To see this clearly, refer to the Glossary. Look at the wheel rather than the disemboweled man. The wheel will more clearly show the proximity of Pisces to Aries.

Capricorn is the last of the suitable signs for extraction or dental surgery. This is not a Mutable sign. It is Cardinal, which in itself is not desirable, but there are other plus factors for the use of this sign: One, it rules the knees, a suitable distance from the site of surgery; two, it is the most practical and staid Cardinal sign; three, Capricorn has a direct connection to the body's bone structure and teeth. This is an affinity that can be utilized.

For these reasons, Capricorn is slightly better than Pisces. But, keep in mind, Capricorn, too, leaves little "healing time" before the Moon has journeyed back to the site of surgery.

Now, very quickly, we will explain why the other seven signs are not satisfactory for extractions or dental surgery. We have already discussed Aries and Taurus, and explained why they were eliminated, because they were too closely involved with the site of the extractions or surgery. But what about the other five?

Cancer is a Cardinal (or active) sign, ruling the stomach, which is very often upset after surgery, and for a variety of reasons, not the least of which is a fear of the procedure, and possibly the swallowing of some of the medications used during the procedure.

Libra, also Cardinal, and therefore active, is eliminated for that specific reason, but it is also eliminated because when work is done in or near the face, the question of appearance always arises. For this reason, Libra is eliminated.

The Fixed signs of Leo, Scorpio and Aquarius are not considered because of that very quality – inflexibility. What is sought here, whether the procedure is an extraction or surgery, is change. But, in addition, Leo rules the heart and Aquarius rules the circulation, so neither of these would be suitable for extractions or any kind of surgery.

Habits

THE RULE: To make a new habit, begin it as early as possible in the 1st Quarter in the sign of Capricorn; to break an old habit, start the process on a waning Moon (4th Quarter preferred) in the signs of Leo, Gemini or Virgo.

To make a new habit you will need all the positive energies possible while that habit is being established. Therefore, the early days of the New Moon (1st Quarter) are advised. In this way you have fourteen or fifteen days before the waning Moon saps energy from your determination.

Capricorn is the first choice, for two reasons: One, Capricorn rules habits; and, two, Capricorn will always reward honest effort.

Breaking a habit uses the reverse procedure: a waning Moon (4th

Quarter preferred, when energies are at the lowest ebb), with the Moon in a barren sign. Leo, Gemini and Virgo are the preferred barren signs, but you can use Aries, Sagittarius or even the semi-fruitful sign of Capricorn. You can readily see that a barren sign is effective. The habit cannot "reseed" itself. There are those that say Gemini, Virgo and Sagittarius are especially good, not only because they are barren, but because they are Mutable, and therefore negative in nature. Why Capricorn, a semi-fruitful sign? As you will recall, Capricorn is the sign that gives only what is earned. If you put forth the effort, she will give you support, but give it a half-hearted effort and you will surely fail.

Hair and Haircuts

THE RULE: To encourage hair growth, cut in a growing Moon (1st or 2nd Quarter) in the fruitful, fertile signs of Cancer, Scorpio or Pisces; to retard hair growth, cut during the waning of the Moon (3rd or 4th Quarter) in the barren signs, with Leo, Gemini and Virgo as preferences.

That's the basic rule. It's all you will need in most instances, but there are variations because of the purpose of the cutting. For that reason there are other signs that may be used to accomplish these special aims.

Before we go into those special conditions, we will quickly explain the theory behind the rules.

By now you are fully aware that growth is best achieved in the 1st and 2nd Quarters, because that is the period of the Moon's growth, the growth of its energies; conversely you know that growth is not encouraged, at least above ground, when those energies are waning in the 3rd and 4th Quarters of the Moon.

And, quite obviously, fruitful, fertile signs, when combined with rising energies, will further encourage growth, just as barren signs, in declining energy, will thwart growth. This point has been made again and again, but it is basic to success in a variety of applications.

Now, what about those special conditions that we mentioned earlier in this section? What if you want thicker hair, a new hairstyle, a color change, or perhaps a permanent?

Beauty is an important factor with most women (and more men than ever admit it), and for that reason the sign of Libra is preferred by

119

many for cutting hair before a new permanent. Getting the hair cut in Libra, though, is only half the battle. You must also choose a Moon phase that will augment your purpose. Choose from the New Moon to the Full Moon (1st or 2nd Quarter) if growth is desired; Full Moon to the New Moon (3rd or 4th Quarter) if growth is to be retarded, as it might be with a new permanent. It all depends on the purpose you have in mind.

Everything you've read in this book has made the point that Aquarius is a masculine, barren sign, and it seems unlikely that we would recommend it for haircutting, but we do make such a recommendation if the purpose of the cut is a "new direction," a new look. We must stress this point, however: Be sure any haircutting in Aquarius is done on a growing Moon, preferably the 1st Quarter. With a barren sign you need the energy of a growing Moon for the health and vitality of the hair. We recommend Aquarius for your "new look," because it's the sign of new directions. We are now living in a period that is at the doorway of the Age of Aquarius – the New Direction of Mankind. Some call it the New Age. So, even though Aquarius is a barren sign, by its very nature, it is a good time for a haircut if your purpose is a new style, or color, or even a permanent.

If the purpose is to thicken your hair, to produce a more abundant growth, try a cut when the Moon is in the 1st or 2nd Quarter (preferably the 1st), in Pisces, Libra or Virgo. You can readily see the reason for Pisces (abundance with healthy roots), and for Libra (for beauty brought about by thick, luxuriant hair), but Virgo! Virgo? How many times have we stressed that this is the barren sign of the virgin, the non-producer. No, we haven't lost our minds. Virgo is not used for any growth where a fruit is to be produced, but, as an earth sign, it can be used for foliage – and isn't that what hair is?

There is the time factor in all of our lives, regardless of our work. We cannot always schedule our trip to the beauty parlor or the barber-shop so it will fall into an ideal Moon phase or sign. The Rule is for the best of all possible worlds. When the ideal cannot be achieved, there are other fruitful or semi-fruitful signs that help to produce growth other than those three cited as most desirable for growth, just as there are other barren signs in addition to Leo, Gemini and Virgo (see Glossary). So, make your appointments as your schedule will allow, but try for the best possible phase in the best possible sign for the purpose you have in mind, remembering, of course, that you do have wide latitude.

Where possible, we prefer the tried and true: For growth, cut hair in a growing Moon in the fruitful signs of Cancer, Scorpio or Pisces; to retard growth, in a waning Moon in the barren signs of Leo or Gemini.

Lawns

THE RULE: To encourage growth, cut in a fruitful sign in a growing Moon, 1st or 2nd Quarter; to discourage growth, cut in a barren sign in a waning or decreasing Moon, 3rd or 4th Quarter.

The Glossary has a list of fruitful and barren signs in descending order. If time is a factor with you, then use whichever fruitful or barren sign most nearly fits your schedule; but, where possible, use the most fruitful or most barren, consistent with your purpose. Unless it is a new lawn, where you are trying to encourage growth, barren signs are usually used, because, at best, in summer, we spend a lot of time mowing. And, as has been said many times, if beauty is a factor, don't overlook Libra as a good sign for an attractive lawn. Libra will not produce as much growth as the fruitful signs.

For inhibiting the growth of your lawn, use a decreasing Moon in the signs of Leo, Gemini and Virgo, where possible; or try Aquarius, Sagittarius or Aries. Please note that Aries is last as a choice for inhibiting lawn growth, and the reason is that Aries is "implied action." This action, combined with a growing Moon can produce growth, so use Aries sparingly if you aim to retard lawn growth.

Painting

THE RULE: Start painting – especially outdoors – in the 3rd or 4th Quarter, in the barren signs of Leo and Aquarius (both Fixed, masculine signs), or in Aries or Sagittarius.

That is The Rule, a thumbnail version, but you do have more latitude. Since most painting is done for beauty as well as utility, our friend Libra may well be considered a suitable sign for starting the job.

Even the fruitful sign of Pisces may be considered because the very act of painting a building – or "painting" a woman, as in the case of an artful makeup job – is the act of disguising, or covering up, or the veiling of flaws. Pisces has this quality; it understands illusion, and all those other behind-the-scene activities that precede any public showing. Painting, therefore, is decidedly Piscean.

Personally, if the job can be fitted into our work schedule, we prefer to begin a painting job in Leo or Aquarius, because these two barren, fixed, masculine signs tend to give better adherence, so that the job lasts longer and looks better.

You have noted, no doubt, that we have said "when you begin" the paint job. We are well aware that some jobs are done in a day or two, but the beginning time is the important factor here. The key day is when the job is "originated." So, when you have a job that will take ten days or two weeks, make the effort to begin the job as early as you can in the 3rd Quarter, and you will have the benefit of that dying Moon throughout most of the life of the project. The Moon phase and sign at the beginning of the job is the most important factor. The rest of it is "job insurance." For further information, see the section in this chapter headed: When To Start Or Stop.

Surgery

THE RULE: Operations are most successful when done in the 4th or 1st Quarter of the Moon, with a preference for the 1st Quarter in one of the signs governing the lower body – knees, legs, ankles or feet (Capricorn, Aquarius or Pisces) – unless the site of the surgery is in the part of the body ruled by one of those signs.

First, the phase of the Moon, and then we will discuss the signs. The 4th or 1st Quarter is preferred for surgical procedures because this is the time when the Moon's phase is farthest from the Full Moon. And, as you know, a Full Moon is avoided because it has a decided influence on the body fluids – in fact, on all fluids on the earth – and surgery during a Full Moon could bring about greater blood loss.

If you live near the ocean, you are well aware of flood tides with a Full Moon. A flood tide is when the difference between a high and a low tide is at its greatest, while a neap tide occurs concurrent with the New Moon, and is a time when this difference in high and low tides is at its smallest.

Whether or not you are aware of flood and neap tides, the Moon affects the "tides" of the fluids within your body in much the same way. The makeup of blood and the makeup of sea water are very, very similar. At Full Moon, therefore, our blood is at "flood tide," and if we are hurt or if we have surgery, there will be more loss of blood. This phenomenon is well known to surgeons and operating room nurses. It may not be a matter of everyday, common knowledge, but that does not make it any less true.

There have been many controlled studies over the years that confirm the fact that bleeding is more intense, that hemorrhaging more prevalent, at the time of a Full Moon, but we will cite only one account. If you are interested, go to your library where more evidence is available. *Time* magazine (p. 74, June 6, 1960) reported that out of 1,000 tonsillectomies, a relatively safe and routine procedure, 18 percent of the associated hemorrhages occurred in close proximity to a Full Moon.

Avoiding a Full Moon may not be absolutely essential for a successful operation, but if you can control the times of surgery, why not avoid greater blood loss? Utilize the two quarters of the Moon farthest from the Full Moon (4th or 1st Quarter), with a definite preference for the 1st, because of the healing that comes from a growing Moon.

So much for the Moon's phases. Now, a look at the signs suitable for surgery, and why these signs are beneficial.

Suppose we start by eliminating certain signs. The first choice for elimination would be Leo. Leo rules the heart, the vital source of life, the blood supply, so avoid Leo for anything other than emergency surgery where there is no choice in the matter.

Avoid the signs of Virgo (the bowels) and Cancer (the stomach), for they, too, though secondary to the heart, are fundamental to supporting life, as are, to a lesser degree perhaps, the lungs (Gemini), and the kidneys (Libra).

So, where possible, you will eliminate, in descending order, Leo, Virgo, Cancer, Gemini and Libra. Keep in mind here that the big no-no is Leo. Avoid Leo.

We have listed Cancer as the No. 3 sign to be avoided, but, as we have pointed out on many occasions, there are differences of opinion. Cancer is one of these. There are people who feel that Cancer need not be avoided (unless it is surgery to the breast or stomach). They feel that Cancer brings a special affinity to the Moon (Cancer is ruled by the Moon), and that, because of this affinity, better circulation is promoted, and therefore, better healing results. These same people are quick to point out that they prefer to have the sign of Cancer occur early in the 1st Quarter, and might avoid it if this were not the case.

So, whether the surgery is on animals or people, avoid a Full Moon, avoid the sign of Leo, and where possible keep the Moon's sign in the lower body. Accordingly, your best signs for surgery, in descending order, are: Pisces, Aquarius, Capricorn, Aries, Taurus and Sagittarius, assuming, of course, that the site of the surgery is not located in the part of the body ruled by the sign in question.

This is an important point, so permit us to restate it so there can be no misunderstanding: *Do not have an operation in the sign that rules that part of the body where the surgery is to be performed.* Which is to say, if you are having a knee operation, never use Capricorn; if it is an operation to the feet, however desirable Pisces is most of the time, never have the foot surgery done while the Moon is in Pisces; if it is surgery to the reproductive organs or the bladder, avoid Scorpio.

Vision

THE RULE: Have eye examinations made in a New Moon or as early as possible in a growing Moon (1st or 2nd Quarter). Use the sign of Libra, Aquarius, Aries or Capricorn.

First, the phases of the Moon. You utilize the 1st or 2nd Quarter to take advantage of those rising energies, so that your examination is done when it will reflect your normal vision at that particular time in your life. The 4th Quarter should never be used. Your eyes are at their weakest during that low energy period and an examination for glasses then could result in lenses that are too strong.

Now the signs. As always, beauty, that age-old factor, is all important. If you must wear glasses (and most of us fight that possibility), then you want glasses that will be attractive. The first choice for the examination would be Libra. Aquarius or Aries would be good second choices because the former concerns itself with vision, with the sense of sight, and the latter rules the head, the location of the eyes. Capricorn would be our next choice because Capricorn tends to reward any honest effort. When you have an eye examination you are making the effort to restore vision or, at the very least, minimize further weakening of the eyes.

When To Start and Stop

THE RULE: To start anything new, begin as early as possible in a growing Moon (1st or 2nd Quarter), with the Moon in a fruitful sign (Cancer, Scorpio or Pisces); to stop an existing situation, begin in the

3rd or 4th Quarter of the Moon (4th preferably – low energy), in a barren sign (Leo, Gemini or Virgo).

When you start a new venture, whether it is a new business, a new habit, a new romance, it is going to require energy, so use the growing Moon, especially the 1st Quarter, and as near the New Moon as possible.

The choice of sign is wide, depending to a large degree on the aim. Capricorn would be a good choice for a new business venture, or even to form some new habit, because Capricorn is concerned with business and commerce, and it also tends to reward the bona fide effort that either of these two ventures must entail.

A new romance – although we don't always have a choice here, and that's what makes romance so eventful – could flourish under the signs of Libra, Taurus, Scorpio or Aries.

As to the ending of existing situations – always a difficult job at best – you will want low energies, so you won't have that angle to fight. Use a waning Moon. The 4th Quarter is best. The barren signs of Leo, Virgo and Gemini are good for any kind of ending, but Aries is also a suitable choice because of the energies it will generate. Capricorn (even though it is a semi-fruitful earth sign) should not be overlooked, because of the reward for honest effort.

Whether starting or stopping a project, the Moon's phase is more important than the sign. You are looking for growth with the former and an ending, a decline, with the latter.

Afterword

There you have it. We've tried to compile a complete source of all the information concerning Moon phases and signs that is available but difficult to find.

We hope this will become a valuable reference book. No one should be expected to keep all this information in his or her mind, but it's nice to know, when a situation arises, that you have a resource available.

The very first copy of the book is our own rough draft. It has been bound with a fiberboard cover. We use it. And, while we are familiar with the concepts, on occasion we still go back to our "first edition" to clarify a point.

To be sure, we have a nice new copy of the published book. It is still pristine, still shining and new. Is it pride that makes us keep our own copy unsmudged? Probably. This may have been a labor of love, but it was, all the same, a labor. In the beginning, we searched out information for our own gardening. As we collected information, we realized that it should be assembled and codified. We found that the job was greater than it first appeared to be.

To see that each chapter contained all the information required for a particular task, we found that some repetition was necessary. A concept can be the same for two separate purposes. We took pains to see that each entity contained the information that would allow it to stand on its own.

As an example, if you had a briar patch that needed to be destroyed, we wanted Chapter 6, Destroying Unwanted Growth, to be the only place you would have to look.

Finally, we want to make clear that much in this book is "folklore," we do not deny it. We found validity in folklore. We now understand why, through the centuries, the Moon's phases and signs have retained a legion of followers.

You are interested in producing a garden with the least amount of work and the greatest amount of harvest. You are interested in a garden that produces food without poisons, one that will not further pollute, and one that will not further erode the natural cycles of life.

Good harvest!

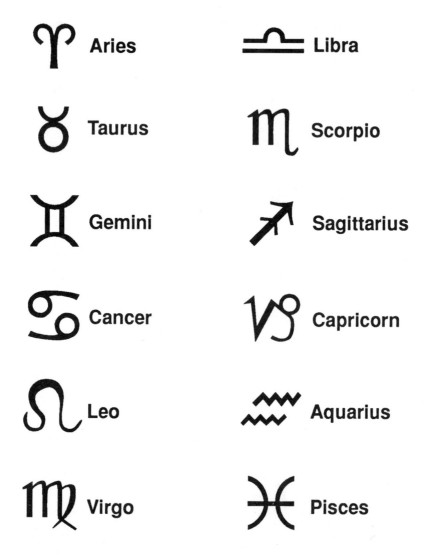

Aries

Taurus

Gemini

Cancer

Leo

Virgo

Libra

Scorpio

Sagittarius

Capricorn

Aquarius

Pisces

Your Tools

Other than your gardening tools (rakes, hoes, tillers) you need only this book and a planting calendar or almanac.

Why an entire section for such a simple statement?

This is why:

Some calendars or almanacs compute the Moon's position in its geocentric place; some compute its position in its astronomic (heliocentric) place. When the Moon's position is computed geocentrically, it's computed from the center of the earth. For planting, this is entirely correct. It's logical. We live on the earth; we'll be planting on the earth. All our activities are "earth-centered."

When computation is made to find the Moon's location in the heavens, as the astronomer does, it is computed from the center of the Sun, or heliocentrically.

Fortunately, most calendars showing the Moon's signs are geocentric, as are most almanacs. But this is not always the case. Because of this, we felt a specific caution should be made.

To clarify, if you compared a geocentrically calculated almanac with one heliocentrically calculated, you'd find that on the first day of January, 1985, the former would show the Moon in Taurus and the latter would show it in Aries. An important – even vital – difference when planting.

The *Old Farmer's Almanac* has been around for over 190 years. We buy it every year, but we do not use it for planting because it is heliocentrically calculated. The editors of *The Old Farmer's Almanac* clearly state their method of calculating the Moon's position in the heavens. They have the correct information for planting on a separate page, covering an entire year. This page of the almanac is headed, appropriately enough, Gardening by the Moon's Sign. And while it does *not* show the time when the Moon enters each sign, it is usable.

Blum's Farmer's and Planter's Almanac, Family Almanac, Farmers' Almanac and *Turner's Carolina Almanac* are all calculated geocentrically, so they are readily usable directly from the calendar pages. Our only objection to these four almanacs is that they do not give the hour and minute the Moon enters a sign.

Another possible problem with your planting calendar or almanac has to do with determining the correct Moon phase. There are four quarters to every cycle of the Moon, beginning with each New Moon. These are sometimes called: New Moon, 1st Quarter, Full Moon and Last Quarter. However, the nomenclature is not consistent from calendar to calendar. The fact is, there are four quarters, so why not refer to them chronologically? (See the Glossary for a complete explanation of this important point.)

Throughout this book we refer to the four quarters by the number of their natural succession: 1st Quarter (New Moon), 2nd Quarter, 3rd Quarter (Full Moon), and 4th Quarter. In this way we believe there will be no question about which quarter is under discussion.

Whatever almanac or calendar you use, be sure that you become thoroughly familiar with the drawings, the symbols and the terminology used in that particular calendar, so you can be sure of the sign. In some almanacs you'll find drawings to indicate the signs (two fishes, a ram, a lion, a bull, etc.); in others you'll find the symbols denoting each sign (see page 128).

It will require a little effort to become thoroughly familiar with the drawings, symbols, or the terminology used by that particular publisher.

In addition, most almanacs will have a human figure, showing the signs, their symbols, and the parts of the body ruled by those signs. The difficulty with these drawings of the "deboweled man" is that from almanac to almanac the terminology is not consistent, although they are all saying the same thing. Libra, for example, may be characterized as "balance" in one book and by "scales" in another. These are the same things; it's just a difference in terminology. And to complicate it even further, Libra, according to most almanacs, rules the "reins," an archaic word meaning kidneys or loins. But whatever the word – be it reins, kidneys or loins – we are still talking about the same area of the body.

130

Another example of this variation in nomenclature is found in Scorpio. The drawing is the scorpion, and, in most instances Scorpio is said to rule the "secrets." That is simply Victorian doubletalk, preserved by the publishers of almanacs, for no good reason. What is meant here is the genitals, the reproductive organs. We have indicated Scorpio's rulership in a more direct manner.

The Glossary has our version of the deboweled man showing the sign, the symbol and all the variations in terminology found in almanacs, both old and new.

We wish you the best of luck and joy as you schedule your daily activities by the Moon's phases and signs.

Glossary

The explanations of the terms used in this book — some of which might not be completely familiar, or which might be confusing because they don't correspond to other source materials — are divided into three parts: Phases of the Moon, Signs of the Moon, and Time corrections for your area.

Phases of the Moon

1st Quarter: That 7-day-plus period of the lunar month beginning with the New Moon. Many almanacs and calendars will refer to this quarter as "New Moon," or they will show its beginning by a drawing of a blackened Moon, indicating that there is no light visible from it on that night. But whatever it may be called, this is the chronological 1st Quarter of the Moon, and it is called that throughout this book.

2nd Quarter: That 7-day-plus period of the lunar month that follows the 1st Quarter and continues until the Full Moon. Some almanacs and calendars show this 7-day-plus period as the 1st Quarter, but you can see how confusing this is, when it is actually the second of the 7-day periods in the lunar month, which always begins with the New Moon.

3rd Quarter: That 7-day-plus period of the lunar month beginning with the Full Moon and which extends for the third of the 7-day-plus periods in a lunar month. On your calendar or planting guide it may simply be titled "Full Moon," but, chronologically, it is the 3rd Quarter.

4th Quarter: That 7-day-plus period in the lunar month before the New Moon. On some calendars or planting guides this may be referred to as the Last Quarter, which indeed it is, being the last of four quarters. But, for absolute clarity, we prefer to call it the 4th Quarter.

Listing the quarters of the Moon chronologically is not a universal practice, and though we are not alone in our preference, we are not pioneering the idea.

Before you begin gardening, before the first seed is planted, be sure you understand the phases of the Moon as they are listed in your almanac or on your planting calendar.

Light of the Moon: That 14-day-plus period of the lunar month when the Moon is growing in light, sometimes referred to as a Waxing Moon, and which corresponds with the 1st and 2nd Quarters of the lunar month. There has always been some confusion on this point. Some people seem to think that the "Light of the Moon" refers to anytime when the Moon is plainly visible. This is not the case. It is when the Moon is in the process of growing in light.

A growing Moon is energized. It is growing in light and energy. During this period of the lunar month, the 1st and 2nd Quarters, above-ground growth of plant life is favored.

Moon phases

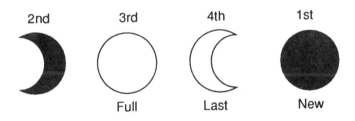

Dark of the Moon: That 14-day-plus period of the lunar month when the Moon is declining in light, sometimes referred to as a Waning Moon, and which corresponds to the 3rd and 4th Quarters of the lunar month. This is the period from Full Moon to the next New Moon.

A waning Moon indicates declining energy. It is decreasing in size. While above-ground growth is not favored during this period, it is a very good time for root crops, or for plants that depend heavily on a root system. This period of the lunar month corresponds to the 3rd and 4th Quarters.

Moon Phase Planting Guide

New Moon 1st Quarter	2nd Quarter	Full Moon 3rd Quarter	4th Quarter
All grains	Beans	Beets	(This entire quarter can be used for underground crops but will not be as productive as the 3rd Quarter. Use only when necessary. Not recommended.)
Asparagus	Eggplant	Carrots	
Broccoli	Melons	Chicory	
Brussels Sprouts	Peas	Potatoes	
Cabbage	Peppers	Radishes	
Cauliflower	Pumpkin	Rutabagas	
Celery	Squash	Onions	
Corn	Tomatoes	Turnips	
Cucumbers	Flowers	Tubers	

You may have noted in this chart that all things planted in the 1st Quarter will seed outside the fruit. The 2nd Quarter is best for things that seed inside the fruit. The 3rd Quarter is for things that produce underground, or that depend heavily on an underground root system. The 4th Quarter is recommended for planting only when it is the only available time.

This is only a partial listing of vegetables. If you understand the theory, then you can determine the best Moon phase for any vegetable or fruit.

The Signs

Name	Rulership	Symbol	Barren or Fruitful	Element	Mas or Fem
Aries	Head	Ram	Barren	Fire	M
Taurus	Neck	Bull	Semi-Fruitful	Earth	F
Gemini	Arms	Twins	Barren	Air	M
Cancer	Breast	Crab	Fruitful	Water	F
Leo	Heart	Lion	Barren	Fire	M
Virgo	Bowels	Virgin	Barren	Earth	F
Libra	Loins	Scales	Semi-Fruitful	Air	M
Scorpio	Genitals	Scorpion	Fruitful	Water	F
Sagittarius	Thighs	Archer	Barren	Fire	M
Capricorn	Knees	Goat	Semi-Fruitful	Earth	F
Aquarius	Legs	Waterman	Barren	Air	M
Pisces	Feet	Fishes	Fruitful	Water	F

From the chart above, note that all fruitful or semi-fruitful signs (planting signs) are feminine, with the exception of Libra. And isn't this a natural thing? Offspring, of whatever type, come from the mothers of the world, plant or animal.

Note, too, that all barren signs are masculine, with the exception of Virgo. And that, too, follows the natural order of things. The father may be the sire, but he is not the producer.

Let's look at those exceptions. Libra, a masculine air sign, should be barren, just as are Gemini and Aquarius. Yet it is considered semi-fruitful, suitable for producing beauty, primarily. The other exception, Virgo, is feminine and an Earth sign, and therefore, should be a semi-fruitful sign, just as Taurus and Capricorn are. Yet Virgo is barren. Now, why is this so? Why these two exceptions, one following the other in the natural order of things? If we look at the one that occurs first, Virgo, we might have a logical explanation. The symbol is the Virgin, the untried, the non-producer. So even though it is an Earth sign and feminine, it is not a producer. Libra is another story, one that was not explained in any of the source materials we explored. But we might offer this explanation: The symbol for Libra is the scales, the balance, the act of weighing, of complete and unbiased fairness. Could not the act of balancing be applied to masculine and feminine? Could not Libra, although masculine, be able to see and understand those things feminine? Is it possible that Libra is almost neuter? It may not be a great producer, but it is good for flowers or ornamentals, for seeds, and for things that produce seeds, such as grain, or any kind of growth where pulp is desired.

The Qualities

Cardinal	Fixed	Mutable
Aries	Taurus	Gemini
Cancer	Leo	Virgo
Libra	Scorpio	Sagittarius
Capricorn	Aquarius	Pisces

The Qualities of the signs are not of major importance for our purposes, but they do add an influence that should be considered when you are trying to understand the "whys" of using the Moon in your gardening or everyday life.

The Cardinal overlay, or influence, is one of action, inauguration, or the act of beginning something. These influences are only of secondary importance, but they are a factor you may wish to deal with when considering the overall sign.

The Fixed overlay, or influence, pretty well describes itself. They give a rigidity to the sign, a desire for establishing something, a determined, stubborn quality.

The Mutable overlay, or influence, is also self-explanatory. These are signs that show a malleable, moldable, changeable quality. Another word might be "adaptable." Years ago, these four were called "Common" signs, but today this word has another connotation, so "Common" was dropped in favor of "Mutable." In either case, if you look at the various meanings of the two words, you see that they share the common denominator of being capable of change.

Rulership Chart

The Signs	Planetary Rulers
Aries	Mars
Taurus	Venus
Gemini	Mercury
Cancer	Moon
Leo	Sun
Virgo	Mercury
Libra	Venus
Scorpio	Pluto/Mars
Sagittarius	Jupiter
Capricorn	Saturn
Aquarius	Uranus
Pisces	Neptune/Jupiter

It is true that these planetary rulers are rarely noted in a discussion of sign gardening. They are included here so that the picture will be complete. We wanted to list all influences.

You can look at this as an affinity rather than a subjugation; an influence rather than an act of coercion. The fact that Libra is ruled by Venus simply adds to that quality of seeking beauty, whether it be in a flower garden or in a fruit jar. And, Saturn's rulership of Capricorn adds to the need for an honest effort to achieve a worthwhile aim.

These are influencing factors, but there is no need to memorize them. Your biggest task is to recognize both the fruitful and the barren signs, and know the parts of the body that are involved with those signs.

Fruitful Signs
(In the order of their effectiveness)

CANCER

The most fruitful of all the signs. Excellent for planting, irrigating, grafting and transplanting.

SCORPIO

The second most fruitful sign. Especially good for any vine-type growth.

PISCES

Fruitful and very productive. Especially good for root crops.

TAURUS

Semi-fruitful. Also good for root crops. Recommended for lettuce, cabbage or anything where sturdy stalks are desirable.

CAPRICORN

Semi-fruitful. This is still another sign that is good for tubers or any other root crop.

LIBRA

Semi-fruitful. Good for flowers, anything where beauty is a factor, and for the seeding of hay, grain or any other crop for the feeding of livestock.

Barren Signs
(In the order of their effectiveness)

LEO   The most barren of all the signs. Use
                           this sign for killing weeds or other unwanted
                           growth.

GEMINI   The second most barren sign. Can be
                           used for cultivating (plowing or hoeing),
                           or for destroying unwanted growth.

VIRGO   Barren. Use for cultivating, weed killing
                           or hoeing. An especially good sign
                           for bringing order to your garden, or for
                           repairing fences and general cleanup.

AQUARIUS   Barren. Suitable for any kind of weeding
                           or destroying of unwanted growth.

SAGITTARIUS   Barren. To a lesser degree, but
                           suitable for destroying unwanted plant
                           life. We do not recommend it, but some
                           people like this sign for planting onions
                           and other bulbs.

ARIES   The least potent of the barren signs,
                           but still suitable for cultivating and
                           plowing where weed destruction is one of
                           the sought-after results.

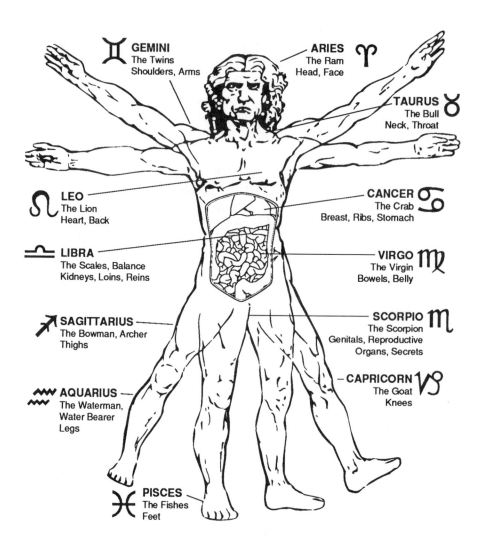

GEMINI
The Twins
Shoulders, Arms

ARIES
The Ram
Head, Face

TAURUS
The Bull
Neck, Throat

LEO
The Lion
Heart, Back

CANCER
The Crab
Breast, Ribs, Stomach

LIBRA
The Scales, Balance
Kidneys, Loins, Reins

VIRGO
The Virgin
Bowels, Belly

SAGITTARIUS
The Bowman, Archer
Thighs

SCORPIO
The Scorpion
Genitals, Reproductive
Organs, Secrets

CAPRICORN
The Goat
Knees

AQUARIUS
The Waterman,
Water Bearer
Legs

PISCES
The Fishes
Feet

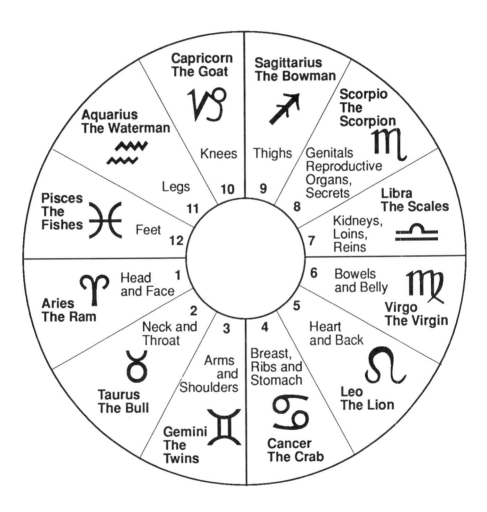

We have included both the familiar "deboweled man" and the circle, which begins at the left-hand side with No. 1, Aries, the Ram, ruling the head and face. For some, the circle is an easier way to see exactly how many signs the Moon will pass through before it returns to a particular place.

As a quick example, the dehorning of cattle involves the head, so we eliminate Aries and one sign before Aries and one sign after it. We eliminate Leo (the heart) on general principles. A barren sign is also preferred for dehorning, so we can do this procedure in the barren sign of Virgo and we will have six signs – six two-and-a-half-day periods of healing – before the Moon will return to the site of the surgery or dehorning, ample time for the healing process to get underway.

When you are looking at the circle, the Moon will be moving in a counterclockwise motion as it goes around the circle. When you are looking at the human figure, you begin at the head (Aries) and move down the figure, going from left to right, i.e., Aries, Taurus, Gemini and so on through the twelve signs.

We apologize if we have put more detail in this particular part of the book than you might be interested in reading, but we know that some people have inquiring minds and are not satisfied with any instruction that says, in effect, "Do it because this is the way it is done." They want to know why, and we think they have a right to know. We suggest that you utilize that part that is useful to you and forget the rest.

Time Corrections

The time the Sun rises in Albany, New York, is not precisely the same time it rises in Cleveland, Ohio, even though they are both in the Eastern Standard Time Zone. Time zones were devised for the convenience of man and, therefore, do not reflect nature. There is a difference of about eight minutes between the true local time of sunrise in these two locations.

This variation also exists with the time the Moon enters any given sign. If you wish to make an accurate determination of when the Moon enters a sign in your own area, then you must determine two things: The place (Time Zone or city) used in determining the entries given in your almanac or planting calendar, and the number of degrees longitude you are east or west of that particular location. With this information, it is easy for you to calculate exactly when the Moon enters a sign in your locality, the true local time.

For this reason, when you choose an almanac or planting calendar, your first priority is to find out which time zone was used in their calculations. (Information always given near the front of the booklet.) The time shown in your almanac is not necessarily the correct time for your particular area. But knowing the time zone or area for their calculations will give you the basis for finding out what the correction will be for you.

As an example, in the text of the almanac you might find this explanation: "Times used are calculated at 0 degrees Greenwich," or, "Times are given for Boston," or "Times used in this almanac are given as Eastern Standard Time."

Now, in those examples, if you happened to live in Greenwich, England, or in Boston, or in some city along the EST 75-degree line, then you would have to do no calculation whatsoever. But if you lived either east or west of that specific point – whichever of the three it might be – you would have to make an easy "adjustment." Since this adjustment stays the same, you only have to make the calculation once. The resulting figure, the adjustment to bring the time to true local time, would be a constant, and could be applied to each sign as it is listed in your almanac.

As an example: The time given in the almanac for their calculations is for Greenwich, England, or 0 degrees longitude. If you live in Peoria, Illinois, you must determine the degree of longitude for that city. You can get this from your library, an atlas, or even from your county agent. Peoria is 89 and a half degrees west of 0 degrees. (Each degree equals four minutes of time.) Multiply this figure (89 and a half) by four, and that is the difference in time (minutes). If you live west of the longitude where the almanac calculations are made, you add this amount of time to the time given; subtract it if you live east of it. In this example, 4 x 89.5 = 358. Each hour has only sixty minutes, so the difference here is 5 hours and 58 minutes, to be *added* to the time given in the almanac, because Peoria is west of Greenwich, England.

Another quick example: Your calendar indicates that it is based on EST. You live in Dallas, Texas. You know that EST is based on 75 degrees longitude, and Dallas is 96:49 degrees. The difference here is 21:49 degrees, or almost 22 degrees. 22 x 4 = 88 minutes, or 1 hour and 28 minutes. Dallas is west of the 75-degree longitude line, so you *add* this calculated figure to the time given on your calendar or almanac.

One last example: Your calendar is based on Pacific Standard Time, or 120 degrees. Let's say you live in Seattle, Washington. Seattle, according to the atlas, is at 122:20 degrees longitude. The difference here is about two and a half degrees. 2.5 x 4 = 10 minutes. Since Seattle is west of 120 degrees, you ADD ten minutes to the time given in your almanac for the correct local time when a change in sign will occur.

THE RULE: Add if you live west of the longitude used on your calendar; subtract if you live east of that longitude.

In the examples cited, each city happened to be west of the longitudinal line of calculation. But suppose you had a calendar calculated for Pacific Standard time and you lived in Denver. PST is calculated at 120 degrees longitude, while Denver is at 105, or 15 degrees east of the PST longitudinal line. In this case you would subtract from the time given. If the calendar indicated that the Moon would enter Cancer at 8:33 a.m. PST, you would subtract one hour from that figure. In your case, living in Denver, the Moon would enter Cancer at 7:33 a.m., 15 x 4 = 60 minutes.

The question is, why bother with these calculations? "If my calendar says EST and I am in the Eastern Standard Time Zone, why should I make any calculations?" It is only necessary if you want to be absolutely accurate. If your calendar says the Moon will be in Scorpio at 8:30 a.m. EST, and you don't intend to plant until that afternoon, then, of course, an adjustment is not necessary. But since you only have to make the calculation once, and since that figure will apply to all signs from that point on, why not be accurate? The gardener living in Dallas who has an EST calculation will only have to remember to add one hour and 28 minutes to any figure given for the Moon's arrival in any sign. No more calculations. That's it. The gardener in Denver using a PST calculation will only have to remember to subtract one hour from any time given on his calendar.

Some people who plant by the signs say, "I never plant on the first day of a sign." This idea has been handed down from one generation to another, and there is a reason for the belief. In the old days, an almanac was the only thing the gardener had to go by, and most of them did not give the time of the Moon's arrival in a sign, just the date of its arrival.

144

In addition, even when the time was known, few people knew how to correct it for their own area. The safest approach was to ignore the first day of a sign, and then you would be sure that it was truly in the sign you intended to use. We believe that is the reason why some people, to this day, refuse to plant in the first day of a sign. Such a precaution is not necessary when you do that simple calculation for your own area.

There is one more problem, also brought about by man's manipulation of time. In recent years Daylight Savings Time has become almost universal in the fifty states. When a calendar or almanac is calculated for EST, it has not taken Daylight Savings time into consideration. So, whether you like it or not, you must add an hour to the time given in all those months of Daylight Savings Time in your particular area. When Daylight Savings Time becomes effective in your area, you move the clock forward one hour, you add one hour, and you must do this if the time on your calendar is shown as standard time.

At first these calculations may sound complicated. Try them; they are quite simple. It only has to be done once. When you know the amount of time to be added or subtracted to correct to your own true local time, it will remain a constant, unless you move. The only other change is to compensate for Daylight Savings Time.

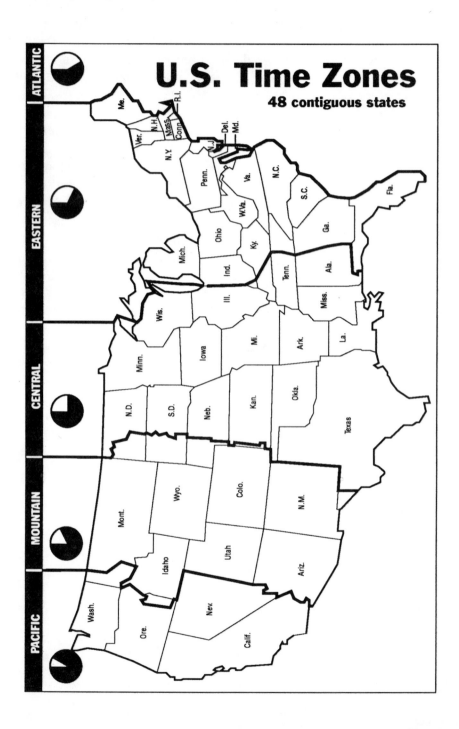

Index